DEEP AND DELIBERATE DELEGATION

A NEW ART FOR UNLEASHING TALENT AND WINNING BACK TIME

DAVE STITT

About the author

Dave Stitt has been coaching executive teams for nearly two decades. Before that, as a civil engineer, he rose to senior management positions in national construction and engineering firms. He has raced in over a hundred triathlons, winning several, and represented Great Britain in the 1991 Triathlon World Championship in Australia. He and wife Sue have two creative sons and live in Washington in the north east of England. He is co-author of *21st Century People Leadership*.

*To my wise bosses Mike, Mike, Brian, Brian and Peter,
who challenged me, let me get on with it and, when the time came,
had the grace to let me go. They didn't need this book. Maybe things
were less complex back then.*

ISBN: 978-0-9567747-1-2

Editing and content development: Rod Sweet
Covers and design: Vanessa Mendozzi

CONTENTS

A NOTE ON GENDER

This book explores dynamics between people, and sketches many scenarios of people interacting, which brought me face to face with a problem that has confused writers since the women's liberation movement got underway in the 1960s. Because the English language does not have a gender-neutral third-person pronoun in the singular, I was forever having to choose 'him' or 'her' when I'd not assigned the hypothetical person a gender or even a name. In former times, writers just used 'him' on the basis that all the important things in human affairs are done by men. Later, writers allowed themselves to use only 'him' on the basis that the reader would of course understand that 'her' could also be used, but that, for ease and consistency, it made sense to stick with one. (Although 'her' was never chosen, that I've seen, anyway, presumably because that would seem 'odd'.) It matters because when we read 'him', our brain supplies a picture of a man, and a picture of a woman when we read 'her', and so to always say 'him' would mean that in the reader's mind the book is populated by males only. My solution has been sometimes to say 'her' and sometimes 'him', quite randomly, to reflect what I hope is the increasingly equal participation of women at all levels in organisational life.

INTRODUCTION:
DEEP AND DELIBERATE DELEGATION

When a long-term client of mine – Mark, the managing director of an international design consultancy – asked me if I would do a workshop for his company on delegation, my response was quite snobby. I didn't do training, I said. What I do is coach executive teams in achieving the results they want. Training in specific competencies I leave to those more qualified to train, I said (meaning that it came further down the coaching food chain). "Oh, okay," said Mark. And we left it at that.

But over the next few days the topic began haunting me. It became a voice in my head that butted into every conversation, such as the one with the manager who complained about the incompetence of her staff. She told me she had asked an employee to do something which she calculated should take an hour, but it took the person four hours and he did it wrong. She and the employee then spent an hour talking about how it ought to be done before she went off and did it herself, which took an hour. Then she spent an hour with her boss discussing the issue, a conversation that produced no constructive result. Added up, the whole enterprise consumed eight hours of company time when it should have taken one.

"You can't get the staff these days," she said. (*"Really?"* said the voice. *"How many opportunities is she giving staff to earn her trust and grow in competence? Is this a staff competence problem or a delegation problem?"*)

In another conversation, an executive said: "I can't think strategically because I'm too busy fighting fires." (*"No, he's hoarding accountability,"* said the voice. *"He should let other people fight fires. And why are there so many fires? This is a delegation problem."*)

"There aren't enough hours in the day," said another executive. "Somehow I have to manage my time better." (*"Hang on,"* the voice said, *"she's an experienced, highly accomplished person. Things take as long as they take. She's doing things others should be doing. This isn't a time management problem, it's a delegation problem."*)

After a few days of this I called Mark back. Yes, I said, I would very much like to do a workshop on delegation because it had dawned on me how bad we are at it and that this is a big part of why organisations have trouble achieving the results they want. "Great," Mark said. Then, after thinking about it for a few more days, I called him back again. "Actually, Mark, I don't think I can do this in a single workshop. There's too much to cover. I'm thinking it will be a four-day programme. Are you up for that?"

"Sure, whatever," he said.

And that's how it all started.

Say 'delegation' and people think of a one-off, linear transaction where Person A asks Person B to do something and off he goes and does it. Simple, right? What's there to talk about? The answer is yes, it is simple, except when it isn't, and it usually isn't. Most often, Person A doesn't ask because she can't work out what she should delegate, or she is reluctant to delegate anything because she wants to protect her territory, or she doesn't believe Person B can actually do the thing that needs doing.

Or, if she does ask, what she asks is open to interpretation, so Person B gets it wrong, proving he can't do it. Or what she asks is too challenging for Person B, so he finds ways of not doing it. Or, having asked, she smothers Person B with scrutiny and instructions so that Person B becomes addled and dispirited and trips up, and has the task taken away from him. Or what Person A asks is boring and tedious for Person B and just adds to his sense of disaffection in work, so he ignores it, or quits. Or Person A doesn't give Person B a deadline or a definition of completion so it all just drifts, to the point where it is too embarrassing for either of them ever to mention again. Or Person A has no direct authority over Person B, so he can ignore the request or merely pretend to fulfil it.

In a clear command structure, delegation is simple. In the armed forces it's called following orders. But in the breadth of organisational life today those circumstances don't apply and neither does the old, one-off, linear model of delegation.

I believe the concept of delegation needs reviving and refurbishing because so many organisations do not do it effectively and they are suffering as a result. Done effectively (in a way I will call deep and deliberate), delegation is the managed process of passing accountability for an outcome from you to another person. It frees you up to do more of what only you can do, what you excel at, and what you really should be doing. But it does something else, too. It is like alchemy because the delegatee, in taking on this new accountability and supported with the right amount of feedback and encouragement, grows in competence and confidence. Talent is unleashed. The base metal of an untested, under-deployed team member is transformed into gold: a new locus of independent, dynamic capability. Deep and deliberate delegation is like cell division: it propagates capability in an organisation, allowing that organisation to accomplish more.

What happens when there is no effective delegation in an organisation? I see it often. Talented and experienced managers burn out while those waiting in the wings get bored and disaffected or are swamped by spasmodic, *ad hoc* task dumping. These organisations are strangled by capability choke points and, from twenty years of organisational coaching, I can tell you that it is the norm not the exception. Mark's request helped me see this. These organisations will make forays into the realm of the possible but, if they are hobbled by ineffective delegation, success is elusive or partial. "Too hard," they say and retreat to the safety of the status quo. They bumble along while the job of accomplishing big things is left to other people, other organisations, other generations.

I believe this is a new problem. It is true that we've always had control freaks and micromanagers. But sub-par delegation is now pandemic, I propose, because in recent decades organisational life has become splintered and is in a state of accelerated flux. Structures that used to mediate between different levels of seniority in organisations have been dismantled. Among the workforce, institutions that used to bring people on in a trade or company role, things like unions and apprenticeships, have withered. The ranks of white collar workers have been stirred up and hollowed out by mass cullings of middle management as companies try and de-layer, believing that process equals bureaucracy, which is fatal for results. Companies have not only taken a chainsaw to perceived dead wood, they've lopped whole limbs off themselves by outsourcing previously integral functions like manufacturing, IT, human resources, legal, even customer service. Organisations' drive to outsource in the quest for their core business has fuelled the rise of self-employment.

Technological change has accelerated the rate of flux because it makes people redundant and disrupts business models, sparking wholesale restructuring and abrupt shifts in direction. Even if a company has been around for a hundred years and has the same head office address, you can be sure there is a lot of head-scratching going on in the boardroom as strategies are re-written, departments are axed, and new ones are created.

Cultural change plays a role as well. Those of us in salaried employment change jobs like never before. My dad worked for one company all his life. I worked for three before starting my own business, and most of my late-Baby-Boomer peers are even more promiscuous: people born between 1957 and 1964 held an average of 11.7 jobs by the time they hit 48, the US Bureau of Labor Statistics reported in 2015. Who knows how many jobs my children will have during their careers? Hundreds, I expect, if they join their peers in the so-called 'gig economy', meaning that sector of the workforce, the fastest growing, who are permanent freelancers – designers, software developers, marketeers, lawyers, researchers all going from project to project.

This splintering means that responsibility for big outcomes is often shared among people who have been flung together, who may report to different line managers, or who may not even be in the same company. Think of product launches, ICT roll-outs, technology start-ups, joint venture schemes, or multi-partner research projects. If you have accountability for an outcome in such a situation, with blurred, fluid or non-existent hierarchies, it's like having to prepare a banquet with a field kitchen you didn't pack. You may be called on to delegate not just down the seniority ladder but horizontally to peers, outward to people in separate commercial entities, or even, as I've seen, up the seniority ladder.

Organisational life as it was when I was born in 1960 has been put into a blender. What it means is that we now often work with people we barely know. Trust is lacking, as is a shared understanding of how things ought to be done, and of mutual responsibilities. It is not easy to hold people to account or to have awkward conversations with them when they are practically strangers. Frustrations between management and staff are left to fester, or workarounds are found. "Oh, we don't hold people to account, we just grumble," as one manager said to me. Usually these frustrations are cast as performance issues – that is, a deficiency in the employee – and are set aside for annual appraisals, even though annual appraisals are notoriously poor at uncovering and resolving real, underlying issues.

Delegation is not a lost art, but an art we haven't really needed before. Our management habits and assumptions haven't kept pace with changing work cultures. Faced with rapid change we struggle as leaders to define what it is we should be doing, and what we shouldn't be doing. Nor is it obvious to us how to trust the people who are available, and with what to trust them. We don't know how to design and frame the outcome we want in a way that inspires commitment and enthusiasm. Having assigned a task, we don't know what distance to keep between us and the delegatee, and veer between oppressive micromanagement and benign neglect. We don't know how to have the awkward conversations we need to have, or to sustain the delegatee with the nutrients of encouragement and challenge. Finally, we pay too little attention to the interlocking systems that buffet us from way out beyond our modest zones of control, believing, wrongly, that the world will sit back and let us get on with it. All of this, I argue, requires mastery of the new art of deep and deliberate delegation.

Executives I work with know something is wrong. Mark diagnosed the problem correctly and I have him to thank for this book. Most, however, believe it is a problem of time management and that with a sterner handling of time they can cram more into their busy schedules. In my view this is a false hope. If important things are to be done correctly, they take as long as they take. Time cannot be managed. It cannot be tamed or improved. It cannot be stretched out or slowed down. It cannot be persuaded or negotiated with. It is a finite, precious resource that marches ever onward, paying us not the blindest bit of notice. There are twenty-four hours in a day and that is that. We cannot manage our time; all we can do is give it away by doing more, or win it back by doing less. For this reason, delegation is a more urgent priority than time management.

The programmes I developed, and which I've distilled in this book, bring together insights and tested techniques that enable you to address all these issues together in a deep and deliberate way. I will show that for delegation to work it must be more than *ad hoc* task dumping, which often misfires and leads to the kind of time-wasting fiasco I described above. Deep and deliberate delegation is a project and a process that requires ongoing participation, feedback and refinement from the two of you – you and the delegatee.

How is this book structured? Part One is about you, the delegator. It asks new questions about how you should be spending your time based on an honest assessment of what you're good at, what you love doing, and what your real priorities ought to be. Part Two switches the focus to the delegatee, setting out how delegation will unlock deep motivation. This part also addresses the tricky issue of trust, and proposes new foundations upon which trust can be built. Part Three looks in greater depth at the thing that is delegated, what we'll call the 'delegation outcome'. Techniques are proposed for framing and articulating the delegation in a way that ensures buy-in, and the astonishing story of tackling child malnutrition in Vietnam is used to explore in depth why it is necessary to let go, how to do it, and all that entails. Part Four, devoted to the art of feedback, shows how to set up stable supply lines through which the right amount of support and challenge flows from you to the delegatee, and through which essential intelligence about the delegation project itself flows back and forth between the two of you and outward to others who need to know. Finally, Part Five, Systems and all that gets in the way, introduces systems thinking and probes ways of increasing your influence over factors beyond your direct control, with a view to supporting the delegatee in realising the outcome you both want.

It might help to hold in your mind this visual representation of the dynamic of deep and deliberate delegation as you proceed through the book.

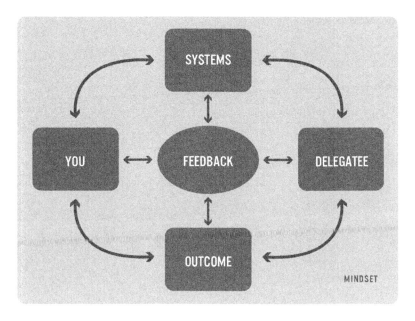

FIGURE 1. The dynamic of deep and deliberate delegation (Credit: Dave Stitt)

Figure 1 shows how delegation, far from being a one-off, linear transaction between two people, is a continuous and multi-faceted process with multi-directional feedback at its core. Each element is giving and receiving feedback from all the other elements. Permeating the process is something I will call 'mindset', meaning thoughts, perceptions, attitudes and mental habits, which matter a great deal. Mindset does not get its own section because it is integral to each of the elements, as we'll see.

What I offer here is not a fool proof, closed system, but rather a set of insights and techniques – some mine, but many developed by coaches and thinkers who are cleverer than me – which, put together for the first time, offer a fresh way of doing delegation that is deep and deliberate, with a view to winning back time for yourself and unleashing talent in your organisation, so that great things are happening – even if it's not you doing them.

PART ONE:
YOU, THE DELEGATOR

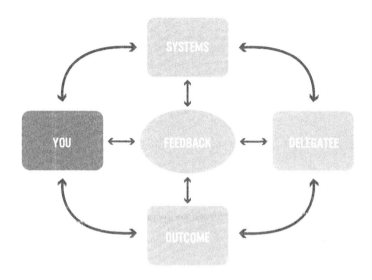

Overview

We start by exploring what it is to be stuck, spinning your wheels halfway up a hill and getting nowhere. The feeling of being stuck is the tension between what is and what could be, and it arises in leaders of teams and organisations who have lost traction. Deep and deliberate delegation is set out as a way for leaders to stop being stuck and to become 'sticky' again, meaning they are able to lure people out of their grooves and enlist them in new, important endeavours. A summary of the top five traits of a good delegator is offered. Then we probe what it is you could be winning back time for by rethinking what it is you should be doing – and what you should stop doing. A subversive idea is introduced: that what you should be doing in your work is what you love doing the most, and what you're best at.

CHAPTER 1
WHY YOU ARE STUCK

If you're reading this, chances are you are responsible for something and you've become stuck. You may lead a team, a business unit, a company or a project, and things need to happen, but they are not happening. You are busier than you've ever been, but the to-do list just keeps growing. Maybe you sense that opportunities are being missed or that risks are looming, but you feel powerless to do anything about this because there is only so much you can do, and nobody else is properly equipped or motivated to do it. "There are not enough me's," you say.

Perhaps you are at a mature stage in your career and you are burning out. Your work is no longer exciting or fun. It may even seem that there is no next stage anymore. Your creation appears to have reached its limits, but it is smaller than you thought it would be. In your mind you can sometimes glimpse and articulate what should be happening, but you don't know how to start doing it and you cannot see the intermediate steps to there. You know you have lots left to offer but you find yourself planning your exit strategy.

Maybe you are the founder of a company or organisation, and you feel you have to do everything yourself because what you built from scratch will be ruined if the people around you get their hands on it. They can't be trusted with anything substantial, you tell yourself, because they are just not as good, as knowledgeable, or as committed as you are. It may even feel like somehow, somewhere along the line, you stopped mattering. Once upon a time you set this whole thing up. You had the vision, the plan, and everybody pitched in to make it happen. Now you're busy, everyone's busy, but your intentions no longer materialise. You are so absorbed in reacting to situations that you have no time for strategic thinking. It's like in a bad dream where you go to smite the monster, but your arm moves so slowly, and with all the force of a moth.

At the other end of the career spectrum, maybe you've recently been promoted and one Monday morning you stop and think, "Can I really do this?" You sense that things may be slipping. You're asking people to take care of this or that but you're not really sure what's happening, or what you may be missing. And then, because you got where you are because of your technical ability and determination, you dive into the task at hand, which feels more comfortable than asking the big questions. You can't shake off a nagging doubt, though: "Will I be found out?"

If some or all of this resonates with you, you're missing something: traction. When I think of the concept of traction, I recall being a project manager building roads through hilly terrain. I had a long wheel base Landrover that could glide up any mucky hill even when it was full of the dignitaries I had to show around the project. During that time, we bought a family car advertised as a semi off-road vehicle, which sounded handy. We used it to take our boys to their Scout camping trip in some rugged moorlands, but when the track got a bit steep and muddy the car started sliding all over the place. I had to get out and push, while the boys watched from a safe distance.

This is what it feels like when you are missing traction: furiously pushing your endeavour up a slippery slope, while your people are watching from safe vantage points.

Inside you is growing a knot of concerns and half-formed ideas. The feeling of being stuck is that knot. It's the tension between what is and what could be. Meanwhile, you are surrounded by people and each one of those people has talents and resources you can only guess at. You can't know all they're capable of because now their role is defined and limited by the status quo – by the way things are done around here. They could help you, but they don't because they don't know you're stuck. You haven't told them, or asked for their help. So, you're sitting there with your knot of concerns and half-formed ideas and they are just sliding by like captains on tankers who don't notice the man down there on the tiny raft.

Maybe you had traction once, but lost it. Maybe the thing you created – the business, department or organisation – has grown beyond your ability to direct all of its parts. It may also be that the relationships that were vivid and strong at the beginning have cooled or become submerged in the excellent processes you set up. Remember how you agonised and argued with your colleagues, how you pleaded and weighed in with support? People are just not available that way anymore. Thanks to your mutual success, they're too busy.

Or perhaps you find yourself in a new situation in which you don't have traction because nobody has any history with you and the bonds that link you together are weak and ill defined, as often happens in our splintering organisational world.

Either way, things need to happen, and they are not happening. You can't just order someone to do the thing because it's not in anybody's job description. That's the problem: often the big thing that needs to happen is new, itself a violation of the status quo. Also, the thing is important and requires more than routine compliance. It needs care, imagination and commitment. You may not even have a clear picture yet of how it can be done.

A way of thinking about this is that you need to become 'sticky' again, meaning people are drawn to you and to your ideas[1]. When you are sticky, people want to be part of your plan and will put their resources to work for it. You need to shake up the status quo and lure people out of their grooves to enlist them in an important new endeavour. To start with, one person will do. That person and you will initiate change. Alone, that person may not be able to do the thing that needs to happen, but together you can begin identifying and taking the intermediate steps. You can get the ball rolling. In one pocket of the organisation you are going to create the conditions that prevailed at the beginning: energy, excitement, commitment.

The process we will explore here is designed to liberate you, not pile on more pressure, which is the last thing you need. I will offer tools that you can use but you don't have to become somebody or something you're not. I will, though, challenge you to think differently about the people around you.

---

1   I've borrowed the term 'sticky' from the authors Chip and Dan Heath who, in their book *Made to Stick*, applied it to ideas. See Chapter 10. I think it can apply to people, too.

Leadership for normal people

When I started thinking about delegation I recalled the mania around leadership that erupted in the 1990s. Fuelled by the dotcom bubble, this fad celebrated leaders as heroes who inspired people to follow them to the Promised Land. It was fun at the time but, in hindsight, much of the thinking exaggerated the importance of the leader himself. A leader could get big things done, so it went, if he was more determined, visionary, ruthless, exemplary, organised and clever than everyone else. Company bosses were urged to emulate Roman emperors, ancient Chinese generals and Arctic explorers. It sounds a bit corny now, but it caught on like wildfire because, I suspect, it fed bosses' egos by inviting them to think of themselves as the centre of the drama.

The problem with the leadership fixation is that it can create unrealistic expectations for people. Most leaders are 'normal'; that is, they are not exceptionally driven, wilful, manipulative or ingenious. I have in mind people who emerged into a leadership role through ordinary ways: a mix of talent, competence, dedication, length of service, diligence, a sense of pride in and enjoyment of what they do, and the fortunate avoidance of disaster. They answered the call. Do they need to transform themselves into philosopher-warriors or Machiavellian princes to get more done? No. Can they accomplish more without twisting themselves all out of shape? Yes, absolutely.

Deep and deliberate delegation moves the focus away from your personal traits as a leader and onto what is more important: the relationships between you and your team.

I call it deep because you will break through the surface of your relationship with the other person whose help you need.

Currently, the interface between you is frictionless. It often amounts to exchanging pleasantries in the corridor. You don't really matter to each other. Your roles are determined by an external process that serves the status quo. A no-man's-land has opened up between you. But now you need to disrupt the status quo. You are going to shake things up.

It's deep and deliberate because it deconstructs delegation as something we pass off now as obvious and hardly worth thinking about. We take it apart and build it back together again as a repeatable method. In our consciousness now, delegation is like a pebble on a beach made small and smooth by rolling in the surf. It has become worn down by familiarity into just a one-off exercise in task dumping. We think we know all about it. But the essentials of delegation are more than that, and they are still there locked in the atoms of the pebble. We're going to crack it open and look afresh at every part of it. We will amplify and reassemble the parts into a process with its own health-checks and feedback loops.

Using it will give you a framework for helping the delegatee grow into new levels of accountability and capability, thereby unleashing the talent that is lying dormant in the people around you. They will become responsible for more, meaning you will become responsible for less. This wins you back time to take on responsibility for more important things, things for which you are really responsible. You will stop being a Custodian of the Status Quo and start being an Agent of Change.

Chapter 1 Reflections, ideas and tools

Reflection • Take ten minutes and allow yourself to daydream about the things that should be happening but are not happening. Write them down. Now, pick the most important. Imagine it happening. Who is doing it? Who notices? Who is affected, and how? And what outcome do you want?

Idea • The feeling of being stuck is the tension between what is and what could be. It is a growing knot of concerns and half-formed ideas. People can help but right now those people, with all their talents and resources, are just sliding by.

Idea • To become an Agent of Change, you need to become sticky, meaning people want to be part of your plan and will put their resources to work for it. You need to shake up settled processes and lure people out of their grooves. To start with, one person will do.

CHAPTER 2
WHAT GOOD DELEGATORS DO

We already know what good delegation looks like. In workshops I ask people to think of somebody who they believe is good at delegating, and then to describe the traits that make them good. The answers are always the same. Good delegators, it emerges time and time again, are people who instil confidence and belief; who are organised; who communicate well; who let people get on with it; and who provide effective feedback. Let's unpack this.

Instilling confidence and belief

The delegator believes the delegatee can do the thing, and inspires confidence in the delegatee by communicating that. When we're confident, we can do anything; when we are not, we are paralysed. And because confidence is like a delicate garden that requires careful tending, the delegator does not just make a declaration of belief at the start, thereafter to commence sniping and criticising, but instead cultivates confidence and self-belief in the delegatee all the way through. Effective feedback is one way of doing that (of which more in Part Four). Another is regularly to measure and appreciate progress as the distance travelled from the starting point, which lifts morale, rather than solely against the desired end point, which deflates morale. The clever delegator instils confidence, too, by framing the thing to be delegated not as a test to pass or fail but as an exercise in capacity development: 'Lessons will be learned, *and* we will get there in the end' is liberating, while 'If you can't do this there is something wrong with you' is debilitating.

Being organised

Having done the necessary groundwork, the delegator understands clearly what needs to be delegated and how it fits into the bigger picture. Accountabilities have been parcelled up in a clear and intelligible way. Priorities have been worked out and the delegator remembers those priorities and sticks to them instead of being blown hither and thither by prevailing winds from week to week. The delegator makes sufficient time available for feedback, shows up on time for meetings with a clear head, able to focus and able to recall relevant discussions that took place before.

Communicating well

The delegator is able to frame the thing that is to be delegated in a clear way, leaving no room for confusion over what success looks like, or by when the thing should be done. Room is given for discussion to clear up any ambiguities. The delegator listens carefully to concerns and responds with due consideration. Furthermore, the delegator conceives and articulates the goal of the delegation in a way that inspires the delegatee, who, as a result, can see the point of the exercise both for the organisation and for him or herself. We explore this in depth in Chapters 9 and 10.

Letting people get on with it

Nothing saps one's confidence and motivation quite like being micromanaged. Having someone breathe down my neck and find fault in everything I do provokes feelings akin to fury, as I imagine a toddler feels at the harsh and arbitrary injustice of having a toy taken away just as the game was getting good. As we'll explore in Chapter 6, people are motivated by a developing sense of autonomy and mastery, so the good delegator practices removing herself to a precise distance, enough for the delegatee to establish ownership of both the process and the outcome. It may take a little longer to achieve the result and mistakes may get made that could otherwise be avoided but they are not likely to be serious and, anyway, some discomfort caused by letting go is the price of propagating new capability.

Providing effective feedback

Letting people get on with it does not mean losing interest altogether. The good delegator retains a stake in the delegated thing and is available to supply encouragement and clarity to the delegatee. There is also a tricky balance to be struck between supportive feedback and challenge (see Chapter 15). We need to learn how to have difficult conversations. Like a coach, the delegator's job is to raise the delegatee's level of awareness of the delegatee's own performance and potential, so that the delegatee can begin to take more responsibility for the factors limiting or enhancing that performance. Good delegation requires active participation from the delegator but not overbearing involvement in the delegated thing, which is why, in the beginning, good delegation does not make the delegator's life easier, necessarily.

As I said, all of this emerges regularly from group discussions, which suggests that we already have an idea what good delegation is. We know, but I would argue that we know in a shallow way, the way most people know they should eat more healthily and exercise more. We may be aware, and we may care, but we also very easily revert to bad habits in day-to-day organisational life. That's why the book doesn't end here. The picture painted above is the tip of the iceberg. Good delegation, by which I mean deep and deliberate delegation, is an art that can be practised and honed. Under the surface are the constituent moving parts, the techniques and insights that can be taken apart, cleaned, oiled and reassembled for reliable use in any circumstance.

One of those parts is a heightened awareness of what you actually do with your precious days, so you can work out what you should be doing and what you definitely should not be doing. The latter is where you look to find things to delegate. I hope you'll be encouraged to hear that part of the answer to the question, "What should I be doing?", is "Exactly as I please!" To that we turn now.

Chapter 2 Reflections, ideas and tools

Idea • Good delegators:

1. instil confidence and belief;
2. get organised;
3. communicate well;
4. let people get on with it; and
5. provide effective feedback.

We'll explore all five in coming chapters.

Reflection • Who do you know that delegates really well? Do they do all four of the above? Do they do other things as well? Which of the above do you already do, and which would you like to improve?

CHAPTER 3
DO WHAT YOU WANT TO DO

Back in 1985, when I was a young site engineer working for a national contractor, I had the privilege to witness first hand a near-perfect act of delegation. We were building a motorway by-pass in the north of England, a job worth around thirty million pounds in today's money. My boss, the site agent, was a talented guy called Ben. He was accomplished, but even he was put to the test in this job. For one thing, it was the company's first road-building project. For another, the locals were dead against it. Although their town was clogged with traffic, the by-pass cut through fields, depriving people of a popular dog-walking route, and it ruined some householders' views. We had protesters lying in front of bulldozers and some town councillors threatening legal action.

Ben took it all in his stride. Bald, five-foot-ten, and with a steady aura of calm, he had a rare knack with people. He handled the protesters politely, made sure nothing got out of hand and that no one got hurt, and forged constructive relationships with home-owners – even persuading one to let us set up our site office cabins next to his property.

But everyone has their Achilles' heel, and Ben was no exception. His was paperwork. Every week he had to submit the Agent's Report, a detailed account of everything that had transpired in the past six days. How many accidents, total staff headcount, which subcontractors were on site, what they were doing, where we were exactly against the programme – all that and more had to be recorded, by hand, on an A3-sized sheet and despatched to head office. This was before the internet, email, and software that automatically captures project information. It was very tedious, basically a Medieval kind of task, except for Tippex and ballpoint pens.

With so much else on his plate, Ben found it to be a real pain, so he stopped doing it.

As one month of no reports turned into three, the telephone messages from his boss got angrier. Head office was completely in the dark about how the project was going. They could tune in to protests on the local news, but from Ben's office came only bland reassurances by telephone. Tension mounted. It was a bit like the film, *Apocalypse Now*, where the Green Berets colonel, Kurtz, becomes a law unto himself in the jungles of Vietnam.

Finally, Ben's boss – we'll call him George – showed up in person. George was responsible for all contracts in the region, and he didn't suffer fools gladly. An almighty row reverberated throughout the site cabin. Why, George demanded, was Ben refusing to hand in any reports? Backed into a corner, Ben's voice rose uncharacteristically. The job was difficult, he shot back, but it was going fine thanks to him, and he'd get to the paperwork when time bloody well allowed. We sat at our desks, open-mouthed. It went back and forth like this a few times before George basically threatened to pull him off the job if he didn't get the reports in. Then George stormed out, slamming the door behind him.

For a long time, there was silence.

By and by Ben's office door opened. We pretended to be busy. He sauntered up to my desk. "Dave," he said, an inviting smile on his face. "Good news. I think you're ready now to start doing the Agent's Report. You pull it together and I'll sign it."

This was unorthodox, but exciting for me. I was a junior on the management team, and very keen. It would give me a bird's eye view of the project. I was already pretty much flat out with my engineering duties but, once a week, I stepped back for three hours to pull all the information together and write it up. Ben was patient, and talked me through it. After about six weeks he was signing off the weekly report with minimal Tippex. Head office was a bit suspicious because they didn't recognise the hand-writing, but they were happy to be getting regular, thorough reports. George realised what was going on, but didn't make an issue of it. He knew Ben could not be replaced easily, whatever was said in the heat of the moment. And me? I grew two inches taller because I was a step closer to realising my ambition of one day becoming a site agent.

Delegation unlocks the potential of teams and organisations because it gives the right people the freedom to do the right things, and I'm telling this story because it illustrates Ben's 'right thing'.

Ben was not really too busy for the paperwork. He just loathed it. It sapped his energy and depressed him. He was drawn instead to what he was good at, what made him happy, and what he thought the project needed most: getting people to work together for a common goal. He didn't set out to cause trouble; he just couldn't help himself. Later on, I asked him, why didn't you just do the reports? "It wasn't the real job," he said, a little embarrassed. In fact, Ben was lucky because he was tuned in to something about himself that many people never discover, and sometimes even try to suppress: that mysterious package of talents and capabilities that only he possessed.

The idea of this mysterious package of talents and capabilities, which we all have, was taken up by the popular coach of entrepreneurs, Toronto-based Dan Sullivan, who dubbed it Unique Ability and built a whole approach to life around it. I am a student and fan of Unique Ability, and suggest that it is a very useful way of beginning to define what your "right thing" is for the purposes of delegation.

Your Unique Ability is the combination of talents, interests and capabilities that is unique to you. How do we recognise it? Four ways: when you are in the zone of your Unique Ability, 1) people admire you because the results are stunning; 2) you love doing it and time flies; 3) it gives you energy rather than sapping it; and 4) you get better at it all the time. Success, insisted Sullivan, comes to people who pay attention to their Unique Ability, define it, and start shedding responsibilities that fall outside it.

This is part of the delegation mindset and it is quite a subversive view. It goes against big notions we absorb from birth, such as that great things are achieved only by difficult toil and that nothing worthwhile is easily come by. Unique Ability turns such notions on their heads. "What if we really each have a powerful natural talent and way of operating in the world that, if properly cultivated, expressed, and applied to the right situations could achieve the greatest possible results with relative ease?" ask the authors of the 2005 book[2] based on the concept. Sullivan has illustrated the idea memorably by pointing out that Frank Sinatra never moved pianos. He didn't worry about lighting, stage sets, or ticket sales. Other people could do those things better. His Unique Ability was singing and, when he was doing that, he was making thousands of dollars a minute.

Ben wasn't making thousands of dollars a minute, but he did make himself invaluable – and went on to become a main board director in the process – by concentrating on his Unique Ability, which was using his wiles to convince people to hitch their agendas to a common goal. I witnessed it many times, and he even used those wiles on me. Several years after the by-pass project, I was on another difficult job (now as site agent!) working alongside a tough old foreman called Leonard. I had huge respect for Leonard, and had learned a lot working under him. He'd started as a labourer and worked his way up through the ranks, gaining a reputation for absolute unstoppability. He once made company legend by pushing forward with a large, technically difficult concrete pour, against both odds and advice, finishing without a hitch – and saving the project schedule in the process – at 5 am on Christmas Eve. But we clashed, possibly because, as an engineer, I would rise faster and higher than he would, or, more likely, because we were each so stubborn. On this particular job the friction between us was getting in the way, and Ben, who was above us both as project manager, called us into his office.

---

2   Nomura, C., Waller, J., Waller, S. 2005-2006. *Unique Ability: Creating The Life You Want.* The Strategic Coach, Inc. Toronto.

"Dave," he said, "with your talent and experience I have no doubt that you could run this job yourself. And Leonard, you've done seven jobs like this already, and I know you could do it, but I am, and we don't have any other jobs for you to run at the moment, so you're fulfilling an important role here. So that's where we are. Now, why don't the three of us have a conversation about how we're going to work this out? What's my role going to be? What's Dave's, and what's Leonard's? What are your concerns, and what all needs to happen? Let's kick it around for an hour."

It worked. The tension was completely de-fused with our pride intact, and we came to an accommodation that allowed the project to proceed smoothly. It was very deft handling on Ben's part. Less-talented managers would either just avoid the issue and hope everything would somehow be alright, or get us in a room, bang our heads together, and demand we shake hands and carry on.

If you already have an inkling what your Unique Ability is, you're fortunate, because many don't. Most people have never had the opportunity, or been invited, even to think about it. Here is a way to start, proposed in Sullivan's approach. Spend some time making a list of all the things you do in your role. Work from your formal job description, but make sure to include all the things you actually do, as well, from training new recruits, to organising away days, to setting strategy. Then arrange this catalogue of activities into four groups:

1. Things you are incompetent at doing: The realm of stress and futility, you really should not be doing it.

2. Things you are competent at, but don't enjoy: You meet minimum standard levels, but others do it better, and it bores you.

3. Things you're quite good at, but have no passion for: From experience you can do it standing on your head, but it doesn't fire you up.

4. Things you excel at, and love doing: Here you are 'in the zone'. It is the realm of Unique Ability, passion and maximum effectiveness.

If you think of these four categories as concentric rings, the first is cold and distant, the Outer Ring Of Rank Incompetence, a place to avoid at all costs. Next in is the Ring Of Dreary Competence; you do not want to linger here for long, either. Getting warmer and closer-in is the Ring Of Passionless Skill, where many of us spend more time than we'd like. And in the middle is the Bullseye of Mastery.

THE BULLSEYE OF MASTERY

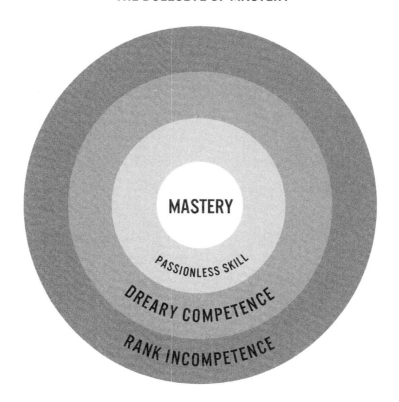

FIGURE 2. The Bullseye of Mastery (Credit: Rod Sweet)

You can make your own visualisation of all that you do by drawing this diagram on a piece of paper and putting every item in your catalogue of activities in the most appropriate ring. Because you get the biggest results when you are playing to your strengths in the Bullseye of Mastery, activities that hit the bullseye or that come closest to it are clearly the ones you want to hold on to, while activities that fall into the outer rings are the ripest for delegation.

This visual map won't tell the whole story, however. We need to add another dimension: time. What do you actually do, day to day and week to week? Many people have only the foggiest notion. For an accurate reading of that I suggest you employ what I call the Time Tracker, a personal time and motion study that tells you exactly how much time you spend on the various things you do. Set your phone or watch to beep or vibrate every hour during your working day. When it does, stop and jot down whatever you're doing at that moment. (Even if it's a meeting. *Especially* if it's a meeting.) Don't think or analyse, just jot it down and move on. At the end of a decent period (two or three weeks, say) you'll have an interesting data set. Say hello to how you spend your time. The point is that extremely busy people often have no clear idea where their time goes because they are too caught up in reacting to emergencies to think about it. One of my clients, a managing director, did this and discovered that he spent 48% of his time on admin! Quite correctly, he thought this was appalling, but the alarming conclusion he jumped to – that his secretary was no good – turned out to be wide of the mark. Doing the Time Tracker will give you a clearer picture of what activities are the biggest time gobblers. The ones that are greediest and farthest from the bullseye represent the fields of activity that most urgently need to be delegated.

Chapter 3 Reflections, ideas and tools

Reflection • What is your Unique Ability? When were you last in your Zone of Mastery, and what were you doing? You are in your Zone of Mastery when 1) people admire you because the results are stunning; 2) you love doing it and time flies; 3) it gives you energy rather than sapping it; and 4) you get better at it all the time.

Idea • Tasks and responsibilities that eat up lots of time and fall farthest from your Zone of Mastery are ripest for delegation.

Tool • The Time Tracker: Do an audit on how you actually spend your working week. Set your phone or watch to beep every hour during your working day for two or three weeks, and jot down whatever you're doing at that moment. Map those onto the Bullseye of Mastery chart to see how much time you spend in the zones of Rank Incompetence, Dreary Competence, Passionless Skill and Mastery.

CHAPTER 4
DO WHAT IS REALLY NECESSARY

Assessing your Unique Ability is a good way to start working out what you should be doing, and what you should stop doing. But there is another filter, which takes the form of an important question: What is really necessary to get your organisation heading where it should be heading?

As a leader your first responsibility is to articulate a vision of where your team or organisation is going. What should the organisation look like, and be doing, in one year, two years, five years? What will we be like, and what will clients be saying about us? Having arrived at the vision, you and your people then need to work out an effective, detailed strategy, a roadmap for getting there. Perhaps this sounds obvious but in practice, many organisations and teams have only the faintest conception of their vision and strategy.

Having a vision is crucial to the delegation mindset. Much lip service is paid to vision and strategy, but there is usually a disconnect between the fancy words and the day-to-day reality. Many executives have admitted to me that their vision is for the organisation to get to the end of the month without calamity or, only marginally more inspiring, not to miss this quarter's targets by too much. One of the reasons for this lack of vision in organisational life is that people rise into leadership roles because they used to be good at what they did. Talented nurses, engineers, teachers, software developers, architects, salespeople, and doctors solve problems, and so get marked for management. Promoted without proper mentoring, however, they can tend to assume that their new job is still solving problems, but on a vaster scale. One chief executive I worked with used to see it as his job personally to sort out all client and technical issues, and would spend his time going from one problem to the next, telling various managers what to do and giving them deadlines by which to report back (micromanaging), all the while complaining about how little time he had for strategy.

That this is a general problem hit me when one manager said in a workshop: "The problem, Dave, is that I know how to do their job" – he meant the job of the person reporting to him – "but they don't know how to do mine." This is profound. The manager knows how to do his report's job because the manager came up through the ranks. But the old job is the manager's comfort zone, so he is still dabbling at it, thereby disempowering his staff member. What this means is that the manager is working one or two pay grades down from his own, and no one is doing the manager's job, unless the manager's boss is also working one or two grades down, in her or his comfort zone.

What if everyone is working at least one level down? It's a sobering thought, and may go some way to explaining the notoriously mediocre standard of management in my country, Britain, which is very good at starting companies but bad at growing them. In 2015, according to *The Economist*, there were just over 608,000 new start-ups in Britain, which is a lot, but hardly any will grow. Fewer than 4% of UK start-ups have ten or more employees after their first decade in existence. These perpetual runts have been dubbed 'muppets' – short for Marginal Undersized Poor Performance Enterprises – by Paul Nightingale, a professor of strategy at the University of Sussex. Compared to Britain, America does better at promoting high-growth companies, which are defined as companies with more than ten employees that grow by at least 20% over three years in revenues or staff numbers[3].

Could a failure of delegation be part of the problem? I believe it is. Good delegation gets everyone turned 180 degrees, so that they are facing the correct direction: onward and upward. A good delegator lets the report get on with it, with proper support, and also draws the report upward, creating 'stretch', and new competence. If the manager's boss is also doing that, we have a stretching organisation.

If you do not have a robust vision for where your organisation is heading, there is an important conversation to be had that falls outside the scope of this book. Suffice to say for now that delegation is essential if you're ever going to have time to a) lift your eyes to the horizon and set a vision and strategy in the first place, and b) do the things only you can do to make the strategy work. Have another look at your Time Tracker. What are you actually doing? Are you arguing with a client over the terms of a contract when you could be out meeting better customers? Are you inspecting scaffolding when you could be setting up a culture of safety in the organisation? Are you negotiating with a disgruntled member of the public when

---

3   'Time to end the muppet show', *The Economist* (2016), December 10–16, page 28.

you could be lunching investors to build confidence in your brand? Are you bogged down in production schedules when you could be meeting the joint venture partner that will open the door to a big new market? Are you sitting in meetings that waste your time?

Ideally there will be some natural overlap between your Zone of Mastery and the things you really need to be doing to steer your team or organisation toward the vision you have articulated. That is the sweet spot, and everything outside it is fair game for delegation. If there is a significant and obstinate lack of overlap, that may be the cue to rewrite your own job description. You need to make the case that the time has come for a realignment of accountabilities so that the things you excel at, the things that only you can do, are being deliberately deployed to help achieve your organisation's goals.

This section has been about you. We've explored what it feels like to be stuck and how becoming sticky again can give you traction in the organisation to begin making necessary things happen. I've introduced the things you'll need to do as you move from being an *ad hoc* task dumper to a deliberate delegator; all of them will be explored in more depth as we go. I've encouraged you to look with new eyes at how you spend your days, and to challenge that expenditure of precious time on the basis of 1) your true strengths and 2) what most needs to be done to move your organisation or team forward. Now it's time to look outward, across the turbulent strait to the far shore, where the other – the delegatee – goes about her or his business, unsuspecting. What do you see? What makes them tick? Can you trust them? Are they up to the job? And, crucially, do they want this? In the next section we look afresh at the people you see every day, the ones who will be your partners in the project of delegation.

Chapter 4 Reflections, ideas and tools

Idea • Being leader of a team, department or organisation should not mean you are CPS (Chief Problem Solver). If you are, you are working one or two pay grades below what you were hired to do.

Idea • Your real job is to conceive and articulate a vision for where your team, department or organisation should be heading, and, with help from your people, to work out a detailed roadmap (strategy) for how to get there.

Reflection • Ask yourself and others what things you can do that will get your 'ship' moving toward the vision, and what among those things fall inside your Zone of Mastery.

PART TWO:
THE DELEGATEE

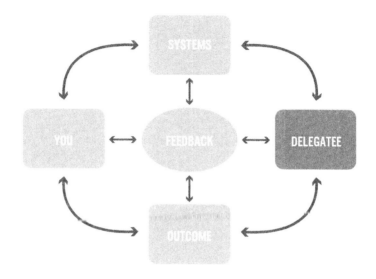

Overview

We start by peeking into the alchemy of delegation: how it is a powerful motivator, offering your employees the rare gifts of mastery, autonomy and purpose. We address the key sticking point of trust. In many reluctant delegators I encounter a big overhang of pessimism regarding would-be delegatees. It would be nice if we had James Bond or the Avengers at our beck and call when we need to achieve a result, many seem to think. But we have who we have. Deep and deliberate delegation does not require you to have blind faith in people you believe are not up to the job, but often the stance of mistrust adopted by many bosses is reflexive, and sometimes based on scant evidence. As a response to this we explore the philosopher Onora O'Neill's astute observations about trustworthiness to help break the trust logjam. This section also contains a tool to help you select the right person to delegate to (or to start working with who you've got), and two meditations on mindsets to help you avoid the self-defeating traps of 1) pigeon-holing people you don't know and 2) assuming that failure is inevitable.

CHAPTER 5
DELEGATION IS ROCKET FUEL

For your team to do something uncommon you need team members who are uncommonly motivated. But how do you achieve that? It is an age-old problem, and solutions have tended toward the bizarre in recent years. I'm thinking about the current flare-up of interest in 'happiness' as the magic bean of workplace motivation. Google and other trend-setting companies have appointed 'chief happiness officers' to inject joy into work. 'Funsultants' are available to help firms spot and defeat outbreaks of gloom with games, unusual perks and team-building exercises. Academics are jumping on the bandwagon. A 2014 study led by researchers at the University of Warwick in England found that groups of workers shown a clip of a comedy film, or plied with chocolate, fruit and drinks, were more productive during a measured period than colleagues who received no such goodies. They concluded that these 'happiness treatments' improved productivity by as much as 12%[4], although they stopped short of recommending that companies try this approach, acknowledging that raising workers' spirits in this way proved both

---

4   Andrew J. Oswald, Eugenio Proto, and Daniel Sgroi, "Happiness and Productivity", *Journal of Labor Economics* 33, no. 4 (October 2015): 789-822. https://doi.org/10.1086/681096

time-consuming and expensive.

To me this feels wrong, as if our emotions were fair pickings for employers to separate out and manipulate in order to get a desired response. Nor does it seem sustainable, especially if an employee's happiness, whatever we take that to mean, relies on external stimuli. What happens when people tire of chocolate or clowns or whatever other diversion a chief happiness officer has dreamt up? Surely, genuine motivation comes from within. The real question should not be how to keep people motivated *in spite of* their work, but how to arrange things so that they are motivated *by* their work.

My cherished guide on this question is Daniel Pink, author of the splendid book, *Drive: The Surprising Truth About What Motivates Us* (Canongate, 2010). Pink challenged the theory of 'scientific management', developed in the late 1800s by American engineer Frederick Winslow Taylor, which held – and I am simplifying and paraphrasing here – that workers are a lazy, unruly bunch who must be managed through rewards (a paycheque, a bonus) for doing what is required, and punishment (fines, or being fired) for doing what is not. Taylor's theory was called "scientific" because it harnessed people's rational drive not to be sacked, to put food on the table and to keep a roof over one's head[5]. Daniel Pink argued that it doesn't work anymore. It was okay in the industrial age when most jobs were routine but now, when success in business requires initiative and innovation, people need something more than carrots and sticks to give it their all.

Money in particular is a questionable motivator, Pink observed.

---

5   Taylor set out his theories in his 1911 book, *The Principles of Scientific Management*.

Clearly, people need adequate and fair recompense, but Pink cites numerous studies showing how money can actually stifle the most important things we want from employees – creativity, problem-solving and commitment. Artists produce inferior work when commissioned. Asked to solve puzzles, people get stupider if you introduce cash rewards. One classic study took three groups of children, all of whom liked drawing in their spare time. Group one was shown a fancy certificate and told they'd get one if they spent the session drawing. Group two were given their certificate as a surprise for drawing. And group three were invited merely to draw, without expecting a certificate or being surprised with one. Two weeks later, children from the second and third groups were still happily drawing, while children from the first group had drifted to other things. Researchers concluded that the expectation of a reward snuffed out their enjoyment of drawing. Overall, Pink said, extrinsic motivation – the promise of money or perks – often promotes short-term thinking, ruins the enjoyment of the activity, encourages short cuts and cheating, crushes creativity and diminishes performance.

Pay is an ever-present issue, but I believe Pink is correct to challenge the primacy of money, or perks, as a motivator. Inadequate pay causes people difficulty and will make them leave a job, even one they love, if a higher-paying one becomes available. But once pay is adequate to a person's needs, as in it provides them and their families with an acceptable standard of living, pay takes on a more abstract value, the numbers comprising our annual salary being a symbol of our worth and achievement relative to others in society. Some people are more anxious about this than others. I used to fret keenly about it as a younger man rising through the corporate ranks. Back in the days of company cars I broke the mould by getting a Ford Escort at the age of twenty-six. It was the bee's knees, but after a week I stopped at traffic lights and someone pulled up alongside me in a Ford Sierra. Wow, I thought: get one of those and you've arrived. Eighteen months later I had a Ford Sierra, and this time the magic lasted for about two weeks, after which it reverted to being just a car, and one on an ever-expanding spectrum of luxury and status.

As a leader you will be limited in terms of how much cash or perks you can dangle in front of your people. Daniel Pink's helpful insight is that it doesn't matter because there are better ways of engendering commitment, excitement and motivation. The trick is to allow for what he calls 'intrinsic' motivation to take hold, where the work itself inspires people. This happens when people are allowed to derive three crucial things from work: a sense of autonomy; a sense of mastery; and a sense of purpose. Happily, for us, deep and deliberate delegation encourages those very ingredients. It is a super-motivator. It is rocket fuel. Let's look at them in a little more detail.

Autonomy is about people regaining control over the discharging of their responsibilities, deciding how they do what they are supposed to do, including the hours they do it in, and the people they do it with. This is anathema to scientific management, which tightly restricts individual sovereignty. Before the Industrial Revolution people worked in a more holistic framework, by which I mean their labours made sense in relation to town or village life. Craftsmen, labourers, smallholding farmers, for instance, worked to deadlines set by the seasons and produced outcomes that were complete, such as mowed field, a shoed horse, or a repaired cartwheel. We don't want to romanticise pre-industrial life unduly, but generally people were brought into play more fully as people, each with unique skills, experience and backstories. Industrialisation took people off farms and put them on assembly lines, there to spend days performing chopped-up, boring parts of much bigger, unintelligible processes. In such circumstances the heart rebels. Reduce people to selling their time by performing mundane tasks and you get perpetual warfare over the minutes of the day: hence the need for scientific management. With machines and computers now taking over routine tasks, people in work should be freer to regain a degree of autonomy over the outcomes for which they are responsible, but managers don't always know how to handle this opening up of possibilities; attitudes rooted in scientific management persist, with battles still erupting over timekeeping, office attendance, and the structure of the working day. As we'll see, good delegation is the orderly restoration of autonomy among the people you most need to have it.

Mastery is about giving people the opportunity to get better at something they care about, not for money or brownie points, but for the joy of it. We step once again into the territory of Unique Ability here, where a person's unique suite of interests and capabilities can find expression in their work. To Mastery, Daniel Pink applies the concept of 'flow', the trance-like, unself-conscious state you enter when you are fully engaged, as is a rock-climber or a sculptor, when the task is only yours to do because your life has shaped you to do it, and it is difficult but alluring at the same time. We delegate to create space both for us to aim for our Bullseye of Mastery, and for the delegatee to discover and cultivate her own.

Purpose gives people a sense that what they're doing has meaning beyond just drawing a salary. Pink argues that the quest for money alone has weakened as a motivator among two key demographic groups: Baby Boomers (born between 1946 and 1964), because they are approaching the end of their working lives and are beginning to feel pangs of the natural human hunger for meaning beyond the satisfaction of their own material desires; and Millennials (people born from the mid-1980s) who seem to want meaning in large doses right from the start, and who are reluctant to step onto the career treadmill merely for the sake of it. Pink finds a growing number of organisations who deploy this appetite in various ways, either by linking profits to charitable works, or by allowing employees to divert some of their skills and time to causes that matter to them. This is good, but I would argue that purpose does not have to mean altruism. The quest for excellence, for the fulfilment of one's potential, and for recognition and honour are equally powerful drivers, even though they could be seen as selfish. In any case, as we'll see, deep and deliberate delegation hands people more control over their careers, giving them the means and opportunity to conceive their own sense of purpose, and pursue it.

Pink finds interesting examples of companies who are trying new things to harness intrinsic motivation, such as the software company that instituted a 'results-only-work-environment', where a requirement to work nine-to-five was dropped, and employees could come in whenever they want, for as long as they want, as long as they got their work done. There is also the 'do-anything-you-want' approach, where employees can use a percentage of company time – 15%, say – to work on a project of their own choosing, the resulting intellectual property staying with the company, of course. Under schemes like this, working all night and cackling away in their cubicles, happy staff produced the Post-It note for 3M, and Google Mail for Google. The famous Mayo Clinic in Minnesota, a healthcare centre, experimented with letting physicians spend one day a week on something they found most meaningful, be it patient care, community service or research, and found this could help reduce burn-out.

Harnessing the power of intrinsic motivation can send a jolt of excitement through firms, Pink says, and it also produces results nobody could have predicted. His crowning example of the relative power of intrinsic over extrinsic is the story of Microsoft's *MSN Encarta*, and its rival, Wikipedia. In 1993 Microsoft launched its bold bid to create the world's first digital encyclopaedia. Expert writers and editors were paid to craft articles on everything under the sun. Microsoft's finest managers were tasked with launching it as a CD-ROM and later as a website, with its premium version available for a fee. Business development people built up revenue streams in online subscriptions, CD-ROM sales and online advertising. It spent millions buying up Funk & Wagnalls and Collier's encyclopaedias. But despite throwing everything it had at the project, Microsoft finally pulled the plug on 31st December 2009, admitting that people just didn't look up information that way anymore. Compare that to Wikipedia. Launched in 2001 by a handful of enthusiasts, Wikipedia by 2009 had become the seventh most visited website in the world, its 16 million articles in more than 240 languages contributed and edited by volunteers, for the hell of it, because it made them happy. The fact that it is powered for free by amateurs – a word derived from the French word for love – remains a testament to the potency of intrinsic motivation.

The experimental approaches to fostering intrinsic motivation that Pink describes are interesting but for many organisations it will be risky and disruptive to roll them out as new-fangled HR policy. Top-down novel approaches usually are. The beauty of deploying intrinsic motivation through deep and deliberate delegation is that you and your delegatee can just start doing it.

By now you'll have had some ideas about things you might delegate. It may be, too, that the faces of possible delegatees have flashed across your mind's eye, and, less encouragingly, that your heart sank. This person is too inexperienced, you may have thought, and that one is frankly incompetent. We're back to square one, it seems: you can't get the staff these days. Except I believe you can. We turn now to the important issue of trust.

Chapter 5 Reflections, ideas and tools

Reflection • Uncommon results require uncommon motivation. What signs of motivation or *de-motivation* do you detect in your team?

Idea • The most powerful motivators are intrinsic: they arise out of the work itself. But still we rely most on extrinsic motivators such as pay or perks.

Idea • People find work intrinsically motivating when it bestows 1) autonomy, 2) mastery and 3) purpose. Deep and deliberate delegation promotes all three

Tool • Further reading: Drive: *The Surprising Truth About What Motivates Us*, by Daniel Pink. Canongate, 2010.

CHAPTER 6
HOW TO TRUST THEM

"If we're recruiting people and we don't trust them enough to delegate to them, then there's a serious question to ask about how we recruit."

This was the frustrated remark made in one of my delegation workshops by a company MD after some of his directors had circled the wagons and insisted that there was nobody – repeat, *nobody* – they could delegate to. Each had at least a dozen experienced people reporting to them. The MD walked to the window, pointed down to full car park the size of a football field, and said: "So they're all incompetent?"

It sounds ridiculous but the perception of incompetence out there among potential delegatees is widespread and deeply rooted, to the point where it is often the default mindset. To me, the MD confessed that for a long time it had been his mindset, too. "All through my twenties and thirties I thought I knew better than anyone else and that nobody had my high standards," he told me. "You get a bit macho, thinking you can do it all. Twenty years on, reflecting on how to get the most from our people, it struck me that they probably have the same attitude now as I had back then." He was right.

Delegation would be easy if we had absolute freedom to pick our delegatee. If you needed someone to launch a winning brand in a crowded market you might go for someone like Richard Branson, the serial entrepreneur. If you needed somebody to set a strategic course for a new business unit, you could do worse than give the job to the uncannily far-seeing investor, Warren Buffett. But this is the real world. We don't have Richard Branson or Warren Buffett. We have who we have.

Sometimes the reason for mistrusting a potential delegatee seems compelling. It may be that they arrived in their current post through a different route than you did, and you suspect that they lack key competencies as a result. Or perhaps the training they received has altered since you were put through the paces, and you feel it is no longer adequate for the demands of the job. A common complaint among older nurses and other practitioners, for instance, is that today's graduates arrive with their heads stuffed with ideas but no practical experience. These sorts of misgivings are understandable, but they are also futile. We have who we have, and blaming education policy-makers will not make them better.

Delegators can break out of this paralysing pessimism by addressing their mindset, for instance by opening yourself to the possibility that the young person in front of you is every bit as intelligent and committed as you were when you began all those years ago. Perhaps mentoring will be needed so that the delegatee can sharpen the skills you arrived with thanks to the training in vogue in your day. That means extra effort and consideration. But it may also be that, thanks to this new training, the delegatee has other skills, such as softer or analytical skills, which you didn't have, and which you may shortly discover you need. In my experience, pessimism toward the delegatee can be genuine, but it can also be reflexive, an excuse, a way for a reluctant delegator to protect her uncomfortable comfort zone, in which she feels safer doing everything herself.

It is important to say from the outset that to delegate is not to perform an act of blind faith. While it is true that in order to delegate we need to place our trust in someone, it should never be a leap in the dark. If anything, we should be hard-headed about trust.

The philosopher Onora O'Neill has spent years examining the issue of trust and, in a TED Talk in 2013, she restored some much-needed common sense to the subject. Trust, she noted, citing opinion polls and the media, is widely held to be in decline, and this causes concern. So, it is assumed that the aim must be to 'have more trust', and 'building more trust' becomes the urgent priority. Rubbish, said O'Neill. Most people actually have a very good handle on trust. Asked if they trust this person or that person, the answer will be shrewd: "To do what?" When it comes to real people trusting other real people, we make complex, sophisticated decisions. We don't keep our children out of school based on some aggregate measure of trust in teachers. We check a school's results and decide accordingly. If we don't know any plumbers, we pick one based on what we can glean about his or her reputation, and if they fix the problem promptly for the agreed price, we call them again. Trust itself is the wrong object of concern. What matters is trustworthiness, and we are all natural experts at judging that. The aim should not be more trust, but more trust in the trustworthy, and less in the untrustworthy.

Now think of your potential delegatees: are they really that bad? Let's find out.

Three criteria are put forward by O'Neill in assessing trustworthiness: competence, honesty and reliability. This is a good matrix. A chef may be competent to the point of giftedness and will never tell a lie but if, during a pre-theatre surge, he is found passed out in the wine cellar, he is unreliable, and the owner will be justified in letting him go. Similarly, a sales manager may be great at the job and deliver consistent results, all while merrily siphoning 5% of your profits off into a secret account in Panama. He is reliable and competent, but dishonest. And in choosing between two accountants to look after my tax affairs, each honest and reliable, should I choose the one just out of university, or the one with ten years' experience in my type of business? Clearly, the latter is likely to be more competent.

To O'Neill's three criteria I will add a fourth – caring – an attribute that encompasses empathy, commitment and a willingness to help. I use these four criteria in a tool called the Trustworthy Tracker, which should help you make an evidence-based assessment of a potential delegatee's trustworthiness. Here is how it works.

The Trustworthy Tracker

Go back to the person who first popped into your mind as a potential delegatee, the one you may have dismissed. Now use this tool, the Trustworthy Tracker, to score them against each of the four criteria of trustworthiness. Under each criterion choose the statement that fits best and give them the attached score.

Caring

- *They seem to have an innate sense for my needs and interests and, without prompting, work toward an outcome that is win-win for both of us (3)*
- *They ask about my needs and interests and will generally take opportunities, when they crop up, to realise common goals (2)*
- *When specifically asked, they will make some effort to accommodate my needs and interests (1)*
- *They are sometimes not receptive to requests for cooperation (0)*
- *Intentionally or not, they sometimes seem to work against my interests (0)*

Honest

- *They tell the truth regardless of self-interest; I always get the full picture (3)*
- *I feel confident they are telling the truth because I have checked on a number of occasions (2)*
- *Sometimes I have to ask questions to get the full picture (1)*
- *Often what they tell me doesn't feel right, or quite match other accounts (0)*
- *It's clear to me they are obfuscating and deflecting to protect their self-interest (0)*

Reliable

- *They consistently do what they say they'll do; my commitments are safe with them (3)*
- *They mostly do what they say, and let me know in advance if they need more time or help (2)*
- *In the end the task gets done, though sometimes after a reminder, and/ or sometimes late (1)*
- *If I don't hassle them it doesn't get done (0)*
- *They never deliver and are immune to pleas and threats (0)*

Competent[6]

- *They exhibit mastery by anticipating what needs to be done in any situation and knowing how to do it intuitively (5 points)*
- *They are expert, responding quickly to a manifest need through a mix of reasoning and some intuition, drawing on a repertoire of rules-based approaches (4 points)*
- *They are proficient, showing good familiarity with the rules, which allows them to calculate a dependable response across most situations (3 points)*
- *As an experienced beginner, they follow rules and instructions and show some ability to adapt to unexpected situations (2 points)*
- *A novice, they laboriously follow rules, and are flummoxed when there is no obvious application of them (1 point)*

---

6   Drawn from the model of skill acquisition set out by Stuart and Hubert Dreyfus

Table 1 sets out the Trustworthy Tracker in table form. (To download a free, printable version, visit the delegation section on my website, www.DaveStitt.com.)

	CARING	HONEST	RELIABLE	COMPETENT
LEVEL 5	They seem to have an innate sense for my needs and interests and, without prompting, work towards an outcome that is win-win for both of us **3**	They tell the truth regardless of self-interest; I always get the full picture **3**	They consistently do what they say they'll do; my commitments are safe with them **3**	They exhibit mastery by anticipating what needs to be done in any situation and knowing how to do it intuitively **5**
LEVEL 4	They ask about my needs and interests and will generally take opportunities, when they crop up, to realise common goals **2**	I feel confident they are telling the truth because I have checked on a number of occasions **2**	They mostly do what they say, and let me know in advance if they need more time or help **2**	They are expert, responding quickly to a manifest need through a mix of reasoning and some intuition, drawing on a repertoire of rules-based approaches **4**
LEVEL 3	When specifically asked, they will make some effort to accommodate my needs and interests **1**	Sometimes I have to ask questions to get the full picture **1**	In the end the task gets done, though sometimes after a reminder, and/or sometimes late **1**	They are proficient, showing good familiarity with the rules, which allows them to calculate a dependable response across most situations **3**
LEVEL 2	They are sometimes not receptive to requests for cooperation **0**	Often what they tell me doesn't feel right, or quite match other accounts **0**	If I don't hassle them it doesn't get done **0**	As an experienced beginner, they follow rules and instructions and show some ability to adapt to unexpected situations **2**
LEVEL 1	Intentionally or not, they sometimes seem to work against my interests **0**	It's clear to me they are obfuscating and deflecting to protect their self-interest **0**	They never deliver and are immune to pleas and threats **0**	A novice, they laboriously follow rules, and are flummoxed when there is no obvious application of them **1**

TABLE 1. The Trustworthy Tracker (© Copyright Dave Stitt 2013)

Now multiply each score. On a piece of paper, it would look like this:

Caring [score] x Honest [score] x Reliable [score] x Competent [score] = total score

Let's say your candidate delegatee is super impressive, and scores top marks. She would get the maximum 135 points:

Caring [3] x Honest [3] x Reliable [3] x Competent [5] = 135

If it is 135, clearly, you need look no further, and you can probably rely on her for much more than you think. However, notice that the scoring scheme drops steeply. If she scores consistently on the next level down, she would receive thirty-two points, as follows:

Caring [2] x Honest [2] x Reliable [2] x Competent [4] = 32

And if she is consistently mediocre, she gets only three points:

Caring [1] x Honest [1] x Reliable [1] x Competent [3] = 3

The reason for this is that Caring, Honest and Reliable are intimately bound up with trust, a delicate and precarious thing, so much so that if candidates score in the bottom two levels of these criteria, their score, unfortunately, is zero. This may seem harsh; more likely, your candidate will zigzag up and down among the top three levels to get a score in the thirties or above, what I call the Zone of Potential. That means they'll have strengths you can build on, and areas in which they might profit from some targeted support.

This is a blunt tool, and is for your own consumption, but it should help you make a more deliberate assessment of your candidate delegatee's trustworthiness. View it as part of your risk management for the delegation, and apply it with an eye on the task being delegated. Also, it can be a conversation starter. If you are disappointed with your candidate's score because they got zero, but you feel it is not a true reflection, consider broaching the topic with her. You could say, "I'm considering asking for your help on a new project but in the process of thinking about it I realised that I sometimes feel that if I don't hassle you, things don't get done. Is that fair?" Make sure you have examples to hand, and ask for her thoughts. Be prepared for a frank conversation, especially if she thinks you may be part of the problem! (This is feedback, which I discuss in depth in Part Four, particularly chapters 15, How, and when, to get tough, and 16, Seven more tips on delegation feedback.)

Run the Tracker on a few people. Workshop participants tell me it helps them see their colleagues differently, often in a positive way. It also helps identify where additional support is needed, or where a degree of challenge or honest feedback could help build deeper trust. Being a responsible delegator means that you will act on any concerns by raising them with the delegatee. Using the Trustworthy Tracker will help you delegate with your eyes wide open.

It can also help you, personally, build trust. In my work trust often arises as an area of concern but it is mentioned only in very general terms. I often hear people say, as Onora O'Neill observed, "We need to trust each other", or "We need to build trust", but when I challenge them to say how, they are often flummoxed. The answer is we should apply the Trustworthy Tracker to ourselves. It is more than just a diagnostic: it points to the things we need to do to build our own trustworthiness, which means we consistently score in the top two levels of the Tracker. We build trust by building our own trustworthiness.

With a heightened awareness of candidates' trustworthiness, you may begin to feel glimmerings of confidence, even excitement, at the prospect of delegating. You may feel nearly ready to appoint a Delegatee Designate. But there's no rush. Before we go further, we need to loop back to you, the delegator, because deep and deliberate delegation is a rare and fragile process. You're gearing up to embark on a journey through uncharted territory with another person, and it's important to be mentally prepared. In the next chapter I'll discuss attitudes and mental habits that will help the both of you.

Chapter 6 Reflections, ideas and tools

Reflection • Delegators can sometimes be paralysed by a reflexive pessimism toward their potential delegatees. Are you? Think of the people around you that you trust the least and jot down why.

Idea • The young person in front of you is every bit as intelligent and committed as you were when you began.

Idea • Demonstrable trustworthiness should be the focus, not the subjective feeling of trust.

Tool • Trustworthy Tracker: Use this to query your pessimism by assessing the potential delegatee's trustworthiness on four metrics: 1) Caring, 2) Honest, 3) Reliable and 4) Competent.

CHAPTER 7

MINDSET: MENTAL HABITS THAT WILL HELP YOU BOTH

People often approach the topic of delegation weighed down with pessimistic baggage. They are pessimistic about their people, pessimistic about the challenges ahead, and pessimistic about their mutual ability to face them. What follows are two short meditations to help you work specifically on mindset and unload that baggage.

Don't fence me in

In workshops I often project onto the wall a map showing the city block we're holding the workshop in, which is usually their company's offices. What's that, I ask? It usually takes a few minutes for people to work out what they're looking at. "Ah," they say, "that's here." I give them some time to make the connection between the picture – a two-dimensional image of lines, words and coloured shapes – and their memories of 'here', the place they come to five days a week, and its surroundings.

"No," I say. "It's not here. Try again." And it's never long before someone rolls their eyes and says, "Okay, if you want to be pedantic, it's a *map* of here."

"Correct," I say.

I do this to make the point that the map is a crude representation, not the actual place. Even the much richer pictures and memories in our heads are not the actual place. The actual place – the buildings, the air, the cars, the light, the people, the sounds – is out there, right now, independent of us, oblivious to us, more complex than we can know; discoverable, but unbounded by our comprehension.

We often make the same mistake with our people, whom we map, or define and categorise, based on early, or partial, or habitual impressions. Think of the new guy who shows up on the first day, keen as mustard, with a new suit and new shoes. As he's walking up the steps, he trips and scuffs his knee, and there is a small tear in his trousers. Scruffy, thinks the boss, when they are introduced. Worried that his first day is not getting off to a good start, and eager to pitch in, the new guy offers to make a cup of coffee. As he is setting it down on the boss's desk, the boss reaches out for it, bumps the mug, and the coffee spills. The boss's irritation grows. Later the boss wants to photocopy something. He goes to the photocopier but finds that the new guy has jammed the machine (which is old and temperamental). By now, the boss has concluded that the new guy is a bit useless; in the boss's mind, a map of his potential has begun to form.

Cartoonish as this scenario is, I propose that we can be as quick to judge. I can, anyway. When I was a manager I had one of my staff, we'll call him Robert, boxed off as a two-million-pound project manager, meaning I had concluded that projects bigger than that were beyond his natural capabilities. I left the company and fifteen years later bumped into him while running a programme for the company he now worked for. Happy to see him, I asked what project he was running now. He gently replied that he was regional managing director, responsible for projects together worth hundreds of millions pounds a year. I may actually have blushed, and I am quite sure that had we still been working together, me as boss, he would still be running two-million-pound jobs.

And what about the 'problem' member of your team? The one who is slow, or difficult, or obstructive? Have we asked why she seems to be like that? Do we understand what's going on in her family life, or how she may be reacting to the management style of the place, or to the ambient work culture? Do we know what opportunities she has been given? What support and feedback? Are we quite certain she really is slow, difficult, or obstructive? Was she like that when we hired her? (We are touching on the subject of systems here, which we'll explore in Part Five.)

I have worked hard on knowing myself for decades. I've been on many courses, done dozens of psychometrics (it comes with the coaching territory) and have had several coaches, all in an attempt to learn, develop and know myself. And yet, at fifty-seven, I wake up some mornings feeling great and other days less so, and I don't know why, and there are other aspects of myself that I have not yet figured out. If I haven't fully comprehended me after all these years, how can I pretend to fathom other people after a brief acquaintance? We categorise and pigeon-hole people because it makes us feel secure. It becomes one of the neat stories we tell ourselves about the world, to make it comprehensible, to map it. It lightens the load of all we have to think about. But actually, we have no idea, or at least I don't.

When I'm in danger of pigeon-holing people, I try and

remember Laura Dekker. A keen sailor from birth – she was actually born on a boat – she got into some trouble with her first solo crossing from the Netherlands, where she lived, to England in May 2009. It wasn't the strong currents, rough seas or heavy shipping traffic that gave her difficulty. Rather, it was the English authorities' response when she sailed her seven-metre cruiser, *Guppy*, into port at Lowestoft. They asked her to stay put and called her father in the Netherlands, telling him to come and pick her up, because she was just thirteen. When her father said, no, she'll be fine, she was put into care. Finally, he came to 'spring' her from social services. He took her back to *Guppy*, waved her off, and flew home.

Then she got into trouble with the Dutch authorities because she had hatched a plan to sail solo around the world. As a pre-ventative measure, she was made a ward of the courts. After some legal wrangling, court supervision ended in July 2010 and a few weeks later, by then fourteen, she set sail alone from Gibraltar. She crossed the Atlantic heading for the tiny Dutch island country of Sint Maarten, in the Caribbean, from where she began her round-the-world journey. Five hundred and eighteen days later (by then aged sixteen) she sailed back into harbour at Sint Maarten, having circumnavigated the globe.

The authorities were acting in what they thought was Laura's best interest but their map of her had been wrong. "They thought it was dangerous," she would later tell an interviewer. "Well, everywhere is dangerous. They don't sail, and they don't know what boats are, and they are scared of them."

The sweet smell of failure

Early in her career, Stanford University psychology professor Carol Dweck did a slightly mean thing. Wanting to explore how children coped with difficulty, she gave some 10-year-olds problems to work on that were a little beyond their ability. The results took her by surprise and shaped her life's work as a researcher. Some of the pupils reacted positively, with enthusiasm and curiosity, while others were devastated. "Their intelligence had been up for judgement and they failed," Dweck told a TED Talk audience in Norrköping, Sweden, in 2014.

The experience led Dweck to develop the idea of two contrasting mindsets that shape our attitudes to our own and others' abilities. People with a 'growth mindset', as she called it, like the positive pupils above, see their intellectual ability as something that can be developed through effort, learning and practice, while people with a 'fixed mindset' believe they were born with a certain amount of brains and talent and nothing they can do will change that. Growth mindset people are the more go-getting bunch. Faced with problems, they engage and persevere. Failure isn't permanent, it's success not just yet. Using electroencephalograms (EEGs) scientists found more brain activity relating to error adjustments among college students with a growth mindset than among their peers with a fixed mindset.[7] Growth-minded people also showed better accuracy after mistakes. Fixed-minded people, by contrast, are gripped by fear. In studies, fixed-minded

---

7   "Mind Your Errors: Evidence for a Neural Mechanism Linking Growth Mind-Set to Adaptive Posterror Adjustments", Jason S. Moser, Hans S. Schroder, Carrie Heeter, Tim P. Moran and Yu-Hao Lee, *Psychological Science*, 2011

students told Dweck and research colleagues that they would likely cheat next time if they failed a test, instead of studying more. And to bolster their self-image after a failure they would seek out someone who did worse than them. Studies also showed that fixed-minded people habitually run from difficulty, so as not to be exposed as somehow deficient.

The good news is that mindsets are not genetic traits like eye colour, but are instead beliefs and thought-habits. You can change them and help others do the same. Over several years, Dweck and colleagues performed a remarkable study at a New York City school among seventh graders, who often struggle with the transition to junior high. The researchers designed an eight-session workshop for all students, teaching them new skills and strategies for learning and studying. But they also assembled another group and among these children researchers promoted the message that their brains were like muscles, and that the more they used them, the stronger their brains would grow. "Students were riveted by this information," Dweck wrote after publishing the results in 2007.[8] "The idea that their intellectual growth was largely in their hands fascinated them. In fact, even the most disruptive students suddenly sat still and took notice, with the unruliest boy of the lot looking up at us and saying, 'You mean I don't have to be dumb?'."

Both groups saw their maths grades fall on hitting seventh grade, but the group taught the growth mindset message saw their grades rebound, while the others saw a continued decline

---

8   Carol S. Dweck, "The Perils and Promises of Praise", *Educational Leadership*, Vol 65, Number 02, October 2007

in grades – despite the extra help with study skills.

Dweck believes that children's mindsets are profoundly affected by how we praise them. What should be praised is not just success and signs of intelligence, but the application of the learning process – the effort, perseverance, strategizing, and resulting improvements. This fosters motivation and a sense for how success can be achieved. If we praise only successful results and other signs of intelligence, we may give the child a temporary confidence boost, but we may unwittingly be fostering a fixed mindset. The result is greater fragility, and a dependence on constant validation. "Employers are coming to me and saying, we have already raised a generation of young workers who can't get through the day without an award," Dweck said in her TED Talk.

A fixed mindset will sabotage delegation. This applies to you, as delegator, and to the delegatee. Remember that delegation is a rare and fragile process. Things will go wrong. If the delegatee sees their abilities as fixed and pre-determined, every glitch and stumble will be taken as evidence of the futility of the endeavour and, instead of trying new things, he will retreat from it, or claim that it is impossible, or even undermine the endeavour to prove its futility in an attempt to salvage his honour. Similarly, if you as delegator have a fixed mindset and believe that your own abilities are pre-determined and, by extension, that you cannot learn and improve, then you, too, will retreat in the face of difficulties. The world will not just stand by and let the two of you get on with it. There will be headwinds, so try and foster a growth mindset to boost your supply of grit.

So far, I've tried to introduce new ways of thinking about you, the delegator, and about her (or him), the delegatee, and I've suggested some alternative thinking habits that might help give you both confidence as you start your important new endeavour. Now the time has come to train the spotlight on the endeavour itself, and address what it is you are going to delegate, and how. This is where leaders of teams and organisations most often get bogged down.

Chapter 7 Reflections, ideas and tools

Reflection • Check and challenge the map you've made of your candidate delegatee. Do you really know what is going on for him and why he behaves as he does? What if you asked him?

Idea • If you pigeon-hole people, you will probably get it wrong: remember Laura Dekker, who sailed solo around the world at sixteen.

Idea • People with a growth mindset see their ability as something they can develop through effort, learning and practice, while people with a fixed mindset believe they were born with a finite amount of brains and talent.

Reflection • Nobody likes to admit to having a fixed mindset, so watch yourself and your team for fixed mindset statements: "We've just got to get through this week." "Our people are too inexperienced." "There's not enough time." "It's down to personality." "It didn't work, so..." "They just have the wrong attitude." "It all boils down to just one thing..."

Tool • Further reading: *Mindset: The New Psychology of Success*, Carol S. Dweck, Random House, 2006.

PART THREE:
THE THING THAT IS DELEGATED

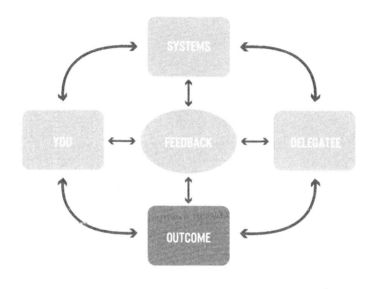

Overview

Letting go of accountabilities can be hard, but if we want to unleash talent and win back time we have to do it. In this section we look in greater depth at the sorts of things you should delegate. Three categories are proposed: Tasks, Processes, and Outcomes. The third category, Outcomes, bestows the most freedom on the delegator and, on the delegatee, the biggest opportunity to grow.

How well the delegation is conceived and articulated affects the quality of understanding between the delegator and delegatee, and the level of buy-in from both. Rigour and precision in language is paramount, so we take a fresh look at the familiar goal-setting technique of SMART. SMART is basic, however. To encourage more ambitious delegation, we explore 'Courageous' goals, and go deeper into how language can be used to secure support for them.

Having articulated the delegation, there are a number of ways a delegator can seem to let go while maintaining a stealthy grip on the outcome. In the final chapter of this section a remarkable case study on tackling child malnutrition in Vietnam is used to probe why it is necessary genuinely to let go, and strategies are proposed for doing that.

CHAPTER 8
TASKS, PROCESSES AND OUTCOMES

At this stage in the delegation programme I usually have to get a bit tough. Busy, responsible people know they need to delegate but when it comes to choosing an actual thing to delegate reflex takes over and they tighten their grip on their kingdoms. Often they try and fob me off with bitty things like "I will ask Parvinder to drive our executive chairwoman to the airport." Sometimes I get cross, imagining a bunch of middle-aged women and men running around micromanaging other middle-aged women and men while complaining that they "can't get the staff these days". But then I remind myself to consider it from their perspective. "This company is my baby, it's just human nature to want to protect it," said one managing director of a professional services firm. "There have been times when my house has been on the line." Nevertheless, I warn people that if they do not get clear on the thing that is to be delegated the exercise will be merely an intellectual one.

Chapters 3 and 4 invited you to think about what to delegate through the prisms of your Unique Ability, and your vision for your team, department or organisation. But having done that, people can still find themselves stuck. One way of breaking the logjam is to ask some trusted colleagues, even ones less senior than you. If you have been hoarding accountabilities you are likely to be surprised at how well developed their ideas are for what you should let go. To be set free you have to delegate something substantial. At a minimum, it should:

1. hurt a bit to give up;

2. feel risky to let go;

3. be stretching for the delegatee;

4. make you all a bit nervous;

5. constitute a good chunk of your time (20%, for example), based on your Time Tracker results (see Chapter 3).

However, we can break it down further. I propose here three categories of delegation, ranging in their impact from modest to intermediate to big, in terms of the freedom and time they give you, and also in terms of the capability growth opportunity they present for the delegatee. At the modest end of the scale you delegate tasks. At the intermediate level you delegate processes. And at the big end, you delegate outcomes. Let's look in a little more detail at each level.

THREE LEVELS OF DELEGATION

LEVEL 1	LEVEL 2	LEVEL 3
Freedom/Growth factor: Modest	*Freedom/Growth factor: Intermediate*	*Freedom/Growth factor: High*
TASK	**PROCESS**	**OUTCOME**
Organise the clients' day at the races this year	Assume responsibility for client outreach	Increase the proportion of repeat business from 50% to 75% by the middle of next year
Do a safety audit on the Birmingham warehouse	Take over health and safety management for the company	Cut the annual number of reportable incidents to zero in two years, and maintain that level
Write this press release	Manage public and media relations	Get us mentioned in the national trade press once a quarter starting next year
Find us a project manager	Look after recruitment	Reduce staff turnover from 35% to 5% within three years

TABLE 2. Three levels of delegation (Credit: Rod Sweet)

Tasks, obviously, are one-off jobs which, transferred from the delegator to the delegatee, frees up time and effort for the delegator. This is entry-level delegation. It is a good place to start and will allow both the delegator and the delegatee (the delegation team) to practise the skills of deep and deliberate delegation – including the art of feedback and systems thinking, both to come. However, accomplished delegation teams will want to move on from this modest level fairly soon. That's because the freedom it affords the delegator is limited, as are the growth opportunities for the delegatee. The task will be done, but then what? You can find another task, or wait until the original task has to be done again. Each time, you'll have to check and feed back on the results. This is serial task delegation, and the supervision cycle is short, loading you back up with managerial responsibilities. Here, too, the method of accomplishing the task is usually prescribed, which can pull you into supervising the method itself, leading to micromanagement. The stop-start nature of serial task delegation also gets in the way of the delegatee developing their competence.

So, the next level up is process delegation, where the delegatee takes over responsibility for an ongoing operational function. If the delegatee did a good job with the task – organising the clients' day at the races, say – maybe it could be time to hand over to her the process of client outreach itself. This is a much bigger responsibility and frees up far more of your time and effort, as the delegatee must set her own tasks, organise her own methods and report on results at pre-determined intervals. I won't be spending much time on process delegation because, in larger organisations, process delegation is usually handled automatically by the promotion of people into more senior roles. But in smaller organisations or teams where hierarchies are fluid, processes are good targets for delegation. Re-engineering a process or creating a necessary process where none currently exists, especially for a young company or team, is a path to glory for the delegatee.

Level three is even more ambitious. Here you're delegating outcomes. So instead of handing over responsibility for a process you're asking the delegatee to use that process, or whatever other means are at her disposal, to accomplish something big. To keep with the example above, it could be to use client outreach to increase your company's proportion of business from repeat customers from 50% to 75% by the middle of the following year. This is a big outcome, and is likely to be very stretching for both you and the delegatee. She must do more than keep a process ticking over. It may be that the process she managed before without much trouble isn't actually designed to achieve the outcome, and needs to be rethought and re-engineered from the ground up. With outcome delegation you cannot hide in the ticking over of processes. As expected results rise higher so does the delegatee's level of accountability. Her job will change and so will the dynamics between the two of you.

The freedom factor for you in outcome delegation is high. You will still be busy, but you will have won back time to do more of what only you can do, and more of what you really should be doing to achieve the vision you've defined for your organisation. Here, too, the potential for unleashing talent by propagating new capability in the delegatee is highest.

It works in the following way. The outcome you delegate should be a crucial part of achieving that vision. Delegating this vision-enabling outcome will mean that both you and the delegatee are now thinking and acting strategically, instead of reactively. You have raised your eyes from the day-to-day grind of processes and have fixed them onto a new point on the horizon. When this happens, all the stuff you both used to do comes under fresh scrutiny. Processes and sub-processes you honoured merely because they were 'what we always do around here' are put in the hot seat and made to justify themselves. Some will get rolled up and redistributed, others will be jettisoned.

Return with me for a moment to our client outreach example. Before, you may have shovelled days of your valuable time organising the clients' day at the races. Then you freed up that time by delegating the task, but you still had to oversee the preparations. Now that you are working toward a new outcome – that is, boosting the proportion of business from repeat customers from 50% to 75% by the middle of the following year – it may be that you stop doing clients' days at the races altogether. Maybe, having spent three months talking to clients, your delegatee has concluded that the repeat clients you actually want don't care about that sort of thing. Instead, she believes that making a number of changes to your service offering will make your company indispensable to them. You weren't expecting that! But it makes immediate sense. So, you begin switching your focus to that and out the window goes the day at the races which, anyway, was a hassle and expensive and was starting to feel ethically dubious, like a subtle form of bribery.

Having explored the three levels of magnitude available to you in deep and deliberate delegation, we must now go back to basics, and take a fresh look at how the thing is delegated: specifically, how it is framed and communicated.

Chapter 8 Reflections, ideas and tools

Idea • To win back time and unleash talent you have to delegate something substantial. You can tell if the delegated thing is substantial if: 1) it hurts a bit to give up; 2) it feels risky to let go; 3) it is stretching for the delegatee; 4) it makes you all a bit nervous; and 5) it constitutes a good chunk of your time, 20% for example, based on your Time Tracker results (see Chapter 3).

Idea • There are actually three levels of delegated things: 1) Tasks, 2) Processes and 3) Outcomes. Tasks are one-off jobs: entry-level delegation. Processes are ongoing operational functions. Outcomes are more challenging, and may disrupt processes, offering the most opportunity for freedom and growth.

Reflection • Stop and think about all that needs to be happening but isn't. If you could delegate one process or outcome that would make a big difference, what would it be?

Tool • If you really don't know what you should delegate, ask trusted colleagues. They are bound to have some ideas!

CHAPTER 9
HOW TO DEFINE IT, AND GET BUY-IN

I confess to being a little wary of bringing up the goal-setting technique known as SMART because, among the organisations I coach, some have been stuffed to the gills with it. However, I also regularly encounter management teams who have never heard of it or who say they know it but then ignore its principles in day-to-day working life. So, because SMART is often preached but rarely practised, and because it is crucial to deep and deliberate delegation, it is worth revisiting this thirty-five-year-old concept.

SMART is an acronym that bundles up the criteria of effective goal- or task-setting. It is generally attributed to a paper penned by George T. Doran and published in the November 1981 issue of *Management Review*, at the time published by the American Management Association. The idea is that to stand a chance of being realised, goals must be:

S – Specific
M – Measurable
A – Agreed
R – Realistic
T – Timed

On three of these letters – M, R and T – I won't spend much time here, because their respective meanings are pretty much self-evident. Measurable means you will be able to tell at a glance whether the goal has been achieved or not, Realistic means it can be done, and Timed means there is a deadline. We'll revisit Realistic in the next chapter, but for basic goal-setting, which is the building block of entry-level delegation, it will do for now. I want to dig a little deeper into Specific and Agreed, though, because it is on these two criteria that even experienced managers and executives most often drop the ball.

First let's examine Specific. What follows is a simple, true story about how we get it wrong.

In one of my workshops I gave the participants some homework. I split them into two groups and asked each group to work together on a short presentation describing their work to the other group for our next meeting, in a week's time. One of the groups had the managing director of the company in it and, unbeknownst to me, when our session was over, he pulled aside one of the other group members – we'll call him Pete – and, before rushing off, said, "Pete, this presentation, could you handle that?" And Pete, an accommodating sort of person, said that yes, he would.

Pete then carved out as much time as he could in his busy week to create the presentation, all on his own. At the next session Pete delivered it, and it wasn't very good: it was rambling, dull, and it left lots of things out. In the feedback session afterwards some of the other group members were annoyed. They complained that they hadn't been asked to participate and that it was supposed to be a group effort. Pete defended himself, saying the MD "told him to do it". But then the MD jumped in and denied any such thing. "I asked you to handle it," the MD said. "Well that's what I did!" said Pete.

In his own mind the MD – a conscientious leader who just wanted to make sure someone was in charge of getting the exercise done – was being as specific as he needed to be. He could picture the task clearly. He might have said: "You heard what Dave said: make it happen." But something got lost in transmission because when Pete heard "Can you handle it?", a very different picture took shape in Pete's mind.

Because 'specific' depends on language, it is subjective and hard to pin down, especially when there is so much management gobbledygook around. You may be asked for instance to 'maximise the synergies between our knowledge-gathering and client-facing workstreams', which sounds grandiose but could mean anything. Turned into plain language it might mean 'get our sales and research teams working more closely together'. Fine, but is that specific? No, it isn't. What does 'working more closely together' mean? How will you know when they are working more closely together, and what will be different when they are? (When a goal is not specific, it will usually fail the other SMART criteria.)

Organisational life today is beset by muddy, imprecise language, and often hides muddy, imprecise thinking. Clear, precise thinking is harder and takes more time to achieve.

I heard a story once about a relatively unknown British novelist being 'discovered' by a famous Hollywood director who was having trouble with a script. The script was for a horror film about a terrifyingly evil supernatural being that wakes up and wreaks havoc on the world. The director had by chance picked up one of the writer's novels and was impressed with the mood of foreboding and suspense he had achieved, so he called the novelist up and invited him over to collaborate. The novelist was thrilled, but the pair of them clashed. The director needed his characters, including his monster, to do things to move the plot along. But the novelist was used to writing about intangible things: thoughts, feelings, perceptions and memories. Although his novel was full of suspense and foreboding, not a lot happened, but in a novel, that's okay.

"So, what does the monster do now?" the director would ask.

"Well, he thinks..."

"What do you mean, he 'thinks'?"

"Well, he remembers..."

"Stop! How am I going to show that on film, the monster thinking?"

It didn't work out. A few weeks later the novelist was on a plane home. He just couldn't adjust to the director's discipline of writing and thinking for visual consumption.

Being specific in goal-setting requires a similar mental discipline (mindset). To keep us on the straight and narrow, I propose the following test for checking the language you use. The Specific Test goes like this:

1. Somebody must do something he or she was not doing before.

2. The 'do' is a good, ordinary verb that a child will understand. If you are not sure, find a child and ask him if he understands the verb.

3. Doing the thing will have a tangible result, one that we want.

Following this recipe means that you as delegator must take the time to think it through and express it clearly. Never mind 'maximising synergies' and 'working more closely together'. Specific would be: 'Get some senior sales people together with some senior research people and have them come up with three useful new product ideas'.

Your closest ally in achieving SMART goal-setting, and hence SMART delegation, will be your delegatee, and this is where 'agreed' comes in. Over the years people have played around with what the letters in SMART should stand for, depending on their priorities at the time. The 'A' has been tampered with most. In Doran's version it was assignable, but other suggested improvements have ranged from 'ambitious' and 'action-oriented' to 'attainable' and 'aligned with corporate goals'. I feel that these mostly miss the mark. Doran's assignable is good because it entails personal accountability for achieving the goal (somebody must do something new). Agreed builds on that in a useful way because the delegatee has to agree, which means the two of you have to talk about it. Talking about it ensures that the delegatee understands the task, and can flag up any issues that might get in the way. Through dialogue you refine the task and make it more SMART. Agreed also leads to better buy-in and a heightened sense of ownership on the part of the delegatee, which is crucial to success.

I class SMART goal-setting as basic. I do that because the R, for Realistic, can tend to set limits on how aspirational SMART goals are. In the next chapter we're going to discuss more stretching types of goals, which we'll call 'Courageous'. But I must stress that there is nothing wrong with SMART. SMART is good. Deep and deliberate delegation takes place on a spectrum that has SMART at one end and Courageous out on the other. The problem is, too many organisations, including those considered leaders in their sectors, do not embed SMART goal-setting as a deliberate technique.

Chapter 9 Reflections, ideas and tools

Reflection • The 'A' in SMART is for 'agreed'. Visualise what the delegatee will look like, what his demeanour will be, when he agrees. There should be some excitement, some back and forth conversation between the two of you as you explore together the specifics and ramifications. There may be some negotiating. Now picture him sitting in front of you, nodding simply to keep you happy and bring the conversation to an end.

Tool • Apply the Specific Test to your language. It goes like this: 1) Somebody must do something he or she was not doing before. 2) The 'do' is a good, ordinary verb that a child will understand. If you are not sure, find a child and ask him if he understands the verb. 3) Doing the thing will have a tangible result, one that we want. (Watch out for weak, weaselly, abstract verbs like 'optimise', 'review', 'oversee' and 'support'.)

Tool • Ask the delegatee to summarise the delegation back to you and listen carefully to the words he uses. Are they specific, and is his 'specific' the same as yours? Challenge the noncommittal words like 'hope' and 'try'; get beneath the surface of his reservations so you can work through them.

CHAPTER 10
WHY IT PAYS TO BE COURAGEOUS

If we think of the techniques and processes of delegation as a vehicle, then goal-setting – the conception and framing of the delegation – is the engine. At one end of the spectrum is SMART. SMART goal-setting is adequate, safe, reliable and good, like the 1.25-litre, 58bhp engine of the classic Ford Fiesta, which will get you from zero to sixty miles per hour in a respectable seventeen seconds. At the other end is Courageous goal-setting, which we might compare to the Lamborghini Aventador, whose 6.5-litre, 1,600bhp engine will get you from zero to sixty in a dizzying two seconds, and whip you along at an illegal 230mph.

Mapping the goal-setting spectrum against the three levels of delegation – task, process and outcome – SMART can and should be applied to all three, but is most comfortable and at home with task delegation, which is a one-off, person-to-person interaction. Courageous goal-setting is most at home with outcome delegation because it tends to generate new, unexpected tasks and bulldoze settled processes. It also tends to draw in multiple people.

Courageous goals are stretching and ambitious. I said that the 'R' in SMART (for 'realistic') can tend to set limits on how aspirational SMART goals are. That is because 'realistic' tends to favour maintaining comfort zones and not rocking boats. It is also an elastic term. What 'realistic' means depends entirely on what is at stake, and for whom: it will mean one thing to someone whose priority is maintaining an advantageous status quo, and quite another to someone faced with losing their home or job. As a coach I am professionally obliged to make the case for unrealistic goals because, without them, a person's or an organisation's potential remains undiscovered and unfulfilled. Without unrealistic goals, progress halts, cures elude discovery and records go unbroken. Delegating a Courageous outcome will help you combat organisational stasis.

We learned from Carol Dweck that individuals can have fixed or growth mindsets. Well, organisations do, too. Often a fixed organisational mindset emanates from the boardroom. In the early 2000s I was asked by a chief executive to help kickstart his company's five-year strategic growth plan. The company was doing okay, but for the last ten years or so turnover had been stuck at £30 million. This was a period of strong economic growth and every other company in the sector seemed to be expanding, so the board was coming under increasing pressure to get a piece of the action. We began the process in the usual way, by getting the board together in a room and asking the basic question – where do you want to be in five years? Two hours later I was wishing I'd never asked because my arm was getting sore holding my marker pen over the white board while they bickered. Back and forth they went. "Well, we could do this but then we'd lose that", and "That's impossible because X, Y and Z", and "What you don't understand is..." Finally, out of frustration, the chief executive stood up and said, "For heaven's sake, give me that pen!" With big, defiant strokes he wrote '£60m' on the board and sat down. There was a brief pause as everybody stared in disbelief at the figure, and then the chorus of grumbles began. "Easy for you to write that!", "Yeah, we're the ones who'll have to do it!" and so on. Three years later, however, the company's turnover stood at £70 million.

Something happens when you articulate a Courageous goal, and it is worth exploring. You start by asking a scary question, such as, what would be the equivalent, for me, of winning an Olympic gold medal? I asked myself that recently and the answer that came back from somewhere inside was: completing a ten-kilometre open-water swimming marathon in four hours, and surviving. As a former competitive triathlete, I'm used to swimming long distances – although 3.8 kilometres is the maximum, and not in open water for twenty years. I still train, but ten kilometres in four hours? That seemed like a massive stretch. Nevertheless, at seven-thirty on a Saturday morning, with the air temperature just 4°C, I plunged with thirty-six other lunatics into the Kielder Reservoir in Northumberland, North East England, and started swimming. Four hours, five minutes and thirty seconds later, I crossed the finish line and staggered up onto the shore without collapsing. I'd done it! I was so happy! For two weeks I was in a state of spaced-out bliss while my fifty-six-year-old body repaired itself from the exertion.

But then I began to think, okay, what's next? What would be the equivalent of winning an Olympic gold medal now? And the answer that came back was nuts: do that again next year – in three hours. This seemed both crazy and very exciting. Crazy, because I thought I'd already reached peak performance. I was in top physical and mental form, and had well-honed techniques. In fact, some years previously, through coaching, I had painstakingly unlearned an ineffective technique developed by habit over twenty-five years, and replaced it with a better technique that increased my speed a little, and enabled me to keep going forever. How was I going to knock a *whole hour* off my time? But it was also exciting because when I looked at it objectively, from outside the perspective of my self-defined limitations, there was clearly room for improvement. After all, I had finished fifth from last, behind people who were older than me and, if appearances were any guide, not as fit as me. With the kind of excitement that makes you get up and walk around, I thought: this is not an impossible thing!

In their book *Challenging Coaching* (Nicholas Brealey Publishing, 2012) John Blakey and Ian Day set out a simple, three-stage process for embarking on Courageous goals. We could call it the Courageous Goal Starter Kit. It's very simple, but profound:

1. Dream it.

2. Declare it.

3. Get started.

I had already dreamt my Courageous goal, so at the next opportunity I shared it by telling the story to participants in a workshop. "Wow," they said, "you swam ten kilometres? That's impressive. Good luck." There was no going back then. When you declare your goal to the world, the world starts watching. I got started by calling my swimming coach, Salka. I explained my goal to her.

"Salka," I said, "are you prepared to partner with me, and do whatever it takes to help me get that result? It means you might have to raise your game because I have no idea how I'm going to knock an hour off my time."

"Dave," she said, "I have no idea either. And to be honest, I'm only slightly faster than you. But this is a good challenge for me, too, and I'm going to ask my coach for advice and do some research to see where we go from here."

I was relieved. If she'd said no, or tried to dissuade me, I'd have had to find another coach who was prepared to commit. I then went to my fitness coach, Mark, and put the challenge to him. Could he help me develop the specific muscles needed to increase my speed?

"I have no idea what those are, Dave, but I'll find out," he said. "In fact, I'll talk to Salka so we can coordinate our training."

Another encouraging response! Everybody was raising their game.

Not long after, something else occurred to me. Maybe I hadn't swum 10km after all. Maybe I had actually swum 10.4km. I'd never worked on the technique of 'sighting', where you look up without breaking stroke to get a visual bead on the buoys that tell you where to go. I was used to swimming in pools, where you just follow the black lines. In Kielder Reservoir there are no lines to follow; you can't even see the bottom. It came back to me how often I'd looked up and had to correct my course. Who knew how much I'd zigzagged around that lake? Maybe just by sighting correctly I could knock a quarter of an hour off my time, or more. An easy win! How many others were there?

This is what happens when you set a Courageous – unrealistic – goal. It forces a scene change. New possibilities emerge and around them cluster new questions, new perceptions, and new relationships. In this way Courageous goals contain their own momentum.

Courageous goals also generate excitement – goal excitement – which is another intrinsic force you can harness. Goal excitement drives action. When someone is excited about their goal they pull out all the stops and need little incentivising. However, there is a dynamic working against goal excitement all the time. Let's call it 'enthusiasm half-life' or 'exponential decay'. Perhaps you've seen it when your team has an away-day and everyone gets along really well; new possibilities emerge and everyone returns home buzzing. But the next day back in the office the boring realities and negative dynamics reassert themselves and, day by day, the goal excitement drains away and the away-day seems like a dream. Worse, the away-day raises hopes and these hopes are dashed and become toxic.

Most teams, departments and organisations have no goal excitement at all, so they need management – inducements by stick and carrot – to battle against enthusiasm half-life. This is why office life is a drudge. Courageous goals create goal excitement in a way SMART goals do not, because the realistic in SMART is self-limiting. But in order to harness goal excitement the goal needs quickly to become real. The team needs to see early action by the leadership, which must also demonstrate, over time, commitment to the goal. Measurable, regular progress toward the goal must be achieved.

In your mind now there may be a Courageous goal brewing.

If so, that is excellent. Pause for a moment, though, and consider the fact that you now have a tough sales job to do, because while you may be excited by it you can be sure others in your organisation will be less enthusiastic. They may even be alarmed because Courageous goals mean change and people find change threatening. You will also battle against simple organisational inertia. The first person you will need to enthuse and enrol in the transformative project is your delegatee. But that is just the beginning. The two of you must then, in effect, start a movement in which many people's thoughts and behaviours change. How you articulate and express your goal will have a big impact on how widely and warmly it is taken up, and for inspiration on this I suggest a formula created by the brothers Chip and Dan Heath in their marvellous book, *Made to Stick: Why Some Ideas Survive and Others Die* (Random House, 2007).

The Heath brothers (Chip is a professor of organisational behaviour at Stanford Graduate School of Business, and Dan is a Senior Fellow at Duke University's CASE Center) set out to answer a profound question: Why are some urban legends, myths, conspiracy theories and memes unstoppable no matter how bogus they are (such as, beware of poisoned Hallowe'en candy!) when worthy ideas that happen to be true so often disappear, making barely a ripple on the public consciousness? They found that really sticky ideas – that is, ideas that spread like wildfire because they are captivating and inspiring – conform to certain principles. There are six, and together they form an acronym, SUCCES. Sticky ideas, say the Heaths, are:

1. *Simple:* The essence of the idea has been so thoroughly distilled that it can be grasped by anyone in an instant;

2. *Unexpected:* The idea violates a schema, and piques curiosity;

3. *Concrete:* Its language is ordinary, and sensory, not abstract jargon;

4. *Credible:* Simple statistics and vivid detail make the idea convincing at face value;

5. *Emotional:* The idea has a charge because it appeals to identity, compassion, fear, or other emotions;

6. *Stories:* Somebody does something, or something happens to somebody – no matter how sophisticated we are, our brains still interpret the world through the medium of stories.

One person who understood this was American President John F. Kennedy. He had a tough sales job when he stood up in front of Congress on the 25th May 1961 to ask for $1.7 billion dollars to fund an ambitious space programme. In his now-famous speech he said: "I believe that this nation should commit itself to achieving the goal, before this decade is out, of landing a man on the moon and returning him safely to Earth." He went on: "No single space project in this period will be more impressive to mankind, or more important for the long-range exploration of space; and none will be so difficult or expensive to accomplish."

This covers most of the Heaths' SUCCES principles, and Kennedy got his money. Had he been a jargon-spouting CEO today, the Heaths wryly note, he'd probably have said something like: "Our mission is to become the international leader in the space industry through maximum team-centred innovation and strategically targeted aerospace initiatives."

Let's look again at our hypothetical example of a stretching outcome: "We want to increase the proportion of repeat business from 50% to 75% by the middle of next year." It doesn't exactly give you goose bumps, does it? We could maybe increase its stickiness if we played around with some of the SUCCESs principles. For instance: "Right now, after dealing with us, half of all our customers go away and never come back. What are we doing to them? This can't go on! We're going to get so good that once they try us, customers stay with us forever." A goal expressed as a dry, corporate abstraction will rarely move people even if it is a great idea. But framed as an appeal to common sense and universal emotions like fear, honour and aspiration, it will do most of the persuading for you.

In the next chapter we're going to explore the difficult topic of letting go of the task or outcome you delegate. But before we leave Courageous goal-setting, a word of warning: just because a goal seems Courageous doesn't mean it is a good goal. Recently I facilitated a programme on collaboration at a large consultancy and afterward the managing partner came to me with an idea for another programme which she said would be "revolutionary".

"I like the sound of that," I said. "What is it?"

"A war on waste," she said.

"A war on waste?" I said. "What do you mean?"

She described what she had in mind, and it was basically to embed a culture of frugality where people turned off lights, brought their own tea bags and scrimped in other ways to save petty cash – a revolution in ground-up cost-cutting that would result in several hundred thousand pounds a year in savings.

It was depressing. I apologised and said that I didn't want to do it. Why not, she asked? I explained that while more rigorous housekeeping to save pennies could be a worthwhile objective there were much bigger fish to fry in the business.

"Like what?" she asked.

"Staff turnover," I said.

Now it was her turn to be depressed.

I knew the company fairly well by then, and knew that staff turnover was high, close to 25%, which meant that roughly a quarter of the fee-earning workforce was leaving and having to be replaced every year. The topic had come up in the programme I'd just run, but only briefly, because it made everyone uncomfortable.

How much, I asked, did she think it cost to recruit a new senior staff member. She didn't know, but made a guess: four or five thousand pounds? No, I said, it's actually round about thirty thousand for a company like this. Recruitment fees, lost intelligence, training for new joiners, time lost getting new joiners up to speed, the lag this creates on projects, the penalties that can result from lags, and from mistakes made as tacit knowledge leaves the building – it all added up. We did some quick maths and worked out that if each loss of a staff member was costing £30,000, the company was losing several million pounds a year because of staff churn.

"So, you can see why I'm not that interested in tea bags," I said. "But I'd love to help you understand why staff turnover is so high and start fixing that."

She was quiet for a while. We both knew this would be a difficult outcome. There were personalities, politics and culture involved.

"Interesting, Dave," she said. "Let me get back to you."

She never did.

Chapter 10 Reflections, ideas and tools

Reflection • Think of a desirable but unrealistic outcome. Why exactly it is unrealistic? Whose comfort zones does it disrupt?

Idea • Courageous goals have their own momentum. They force a change of scene, raise entirely new questions, and call new relationships into being.

Tool • Use the Courageous Goal Starter Kit to get things moving: 1) Dream it, 2) Declare it, and 3) Get started.

Tool • Make it sticky with SUCCES: Get more buy-in for your Courageous outcome by describing it using the principles defined by Chip and Dan Heath and their acronym, SUCCES – it should be 1) Simple, 2) Unexpected, 3) Concrete, 4) Credible, 5) Emotional, and 6) contain a Story.

CHAPTER 11
WHY YOU MUST REALLY LET GO, AND HOW TO DO IT

In 1991, the husband-and-wife team of Jerry and Monique Sternin faced a gargantuan challenge: they had just six months to find a solution to the widespread problem of child malnutrition in Vietnam. The country was struggling to feed itself. It had been just fifteen years since the reunification of North and South after two decades of deadly war, and development was hampered by a US-led economic embargo. The government had dismantled the collective farming system, leaving families without subsidies, and fertilisers no longer arrived from the Soviet Union, itself in the process of collapsing. Vietnam's public health system was a mess and, to compound people's misery, their staple crop had been decimated by a series of typhoons. Around 65% of all children under the age of five suffered from malnutrition.

Somewhat reluctantly, the government of Vietnam asked the American group Save the Children if it could help, and Jerry Sternin, who worked for the organisation, accepted the invitation and moved his family to Hanoi. Given recent history, however, the government had strongly mixed feelings about Americans helping the country, and the Sternins were given an almost self-defeating ultimatum: if they did not show substantial progress in fixing the problem within six months, they would have to leave. On top of that, the solution had to be sustainable. Vietnam could not afford to ship in supplemental food supplies forever: communities had to begin looking after themselves.

Many rational people would have walked away from the challenge. To fix this problem, it would seem that you had to fix the entire country, transforming its agriculture, transport, education and market systems overnight. But the Sternins took it on because they had an idea. The previous year a Tufts University professor called Marian Zeitlin had published studies from around the world showing how some children in poverty escaped malnourishment when the majority of their peers did not. The Sternins believed that lessons could be learned from these statistical outliers – or 'positive deviants' – and spread around to help everybody, and they set out to test the hypothesis in Vietnam. [9]

For their pilot they chose a district seventy-five miles south of Hanoi because it was particularly poor and densely populated. When they got there and explained the approach, local government bosses were less than pleased that this rich American group brought only an idea, and not expensive medical equipment and emergency food supplies. But the Sternins found support among local networks of farmers, women's groups and public health workers, and they assembled a task force of volunteers to get started. They weighed all children under the age of three, and found that 64% of them suffered from

---

9   Read more in their book, *The Power of Positive Deviance*, by Richard T. Pascale, Jerry Sternin and Monique Sternin. Harvard Business Press, 2010.

malnutrition to some degree. Then they did a socio-economic ranking of families to split them into categories: poor, very poor, and very, very poor. All this took precious time, but by the end of the second month they had established that there were indeed healthy children (positive deviants) among the very, very poor families – a promising sign for their hypothesis.

Over the next two weeks volunteers conducted intensive group discussions among the villages, where parents, grandparents, carers and older siblings talked about how they fed and cared for their toddlers. The results were not encouraging. Everybody seemed to be doing the same thing. Changing tack, the Sternins and the volunteers identified six very, very poor families whose children were healthy and, over two days, they visited them in their homes to observe how they fed their children. At last, they found what they were looking for. These families were doing a number of positively deviant things that others were not. As well as the staple, rice, these families were feeding their children tiny shrimps, snails and crabs, and the greens of sweet potatoes, all freely available but not generally considered appropriate for children. They were also feeding their children four or five times throughout the day, as opposed to just twice – once in the morning before the parents went off to work in the rice paddies and again in the evening when they got home. By instructing siblings or grandparents to feed little and often, positively deviant parents were making sure their children, whose little stomachs baulked at large, twice-daily helpings of rice, were consuming all of their daily ration and not leaving any in their bowls. This was the eureka! moment, and it had required patient observation. The positively deviant behaviours didn't come out in the group discussions because the successful parents hadn't thought to mention them, or were shy about them, or the volunteers hadn't listened carefully enough.

Whatever the reason, with the visa clock ticking away, the volunteer task force went into overdrive to make the deviant behaviours the new norm. Families with malnourished children were paired up with the positive deviants to learn new recipes and practices. Two-week-long nutrition rehabilitation courses were designed and rolled out among villages, with children and families graduating at the end. Every day during the course someone from the home had to go out into the paddies with a net and a tin can to collect the day's free supply of shrimps and crabs, a chore that then became a habit. Village health committees monitored children's weight and published charts in village squares, with improvements drawing cheers as if they were Olympics scoreboards.

Judgement day came in June 1991. Six months to the day after the Sternins landed in the country, district health officials fanned out among the villages to weigh the children. Anxiously, the volunteer task force waited in a tiny health centre. Finally, the officials arrived with their results, and they had smiles on their faces. More than 40% of those who had participated in the program – 245 children – had been rehabilitated, with another 20% having graduated out of severe malnutrition. It was enough to get the Sternins another six-month visa. In fact, they didn't leave Vietnam until 1996, by which time the Positive Deviance approach was being rolled out across the country.

This astonishing story illustrates a number of concepts that will help the delegator truly let go of the thing that is delegated.

This is important because, having articulated the delegation, a delegator can seem to let go while maintaining a stealthy grip on the process. I should say that what follows applies specifically to the higher-level delegation of outcomes, as opposed to the entry-level delegation of tasks. First we'll explore the difference between 'complicated' and 'complex' problems or outcomes. Tackling child malnutrition in Vietnam is complex, as are most ambitious outcomes and, as we'll see, the delegator must give the delegatee autonomy in order to achieve them.

Complicated versus complex

We delegate because we want to solve a problem or achieve a result. In this, the Positive Deviance approach is counter-intuitive. It goes against how most of us are conditioned to approach problem-solving, which is to define the problem or the result we want, and then to construct a solution that is equal to the problem in terms of its scale and detail. You can do this with complicated problems, but not with complex problems.

What's the difference? A Swiss watch is complicated. Take the back off one and you will see an amazing feat of engineering. All those tiny springs, cogs and levers operating perfectly in unison to tell time with near absolute precision over periods of many years. The challenge of fitting all that know-how and capability into such a small space will have seemed impossible centuries ago to watchmakers, but it is possible, and the techniques for doing it are known and repeatable. The problem is complicated, but it has been solved.

Complex problems, on the other hand, like tackling

malnutrition (or ending a civil war, or boosting literacy, or pleasing customers), are very different. Complex problems have not been solved and may never be, completely. They have multiple causes and moving parts, over which no one has total command. The physical, political and social contexts of a complex problem are in flux. The actors and agents (individuals, governments, interest groups) are not predictable and have competing, evolving agendas. The system of a complex problem is non-linear, meaning there is no direct correlation between what you do to it (inputs) and what comes out the other end (outputs).[10] Unlike a Swiss watch, nothing quite like it has ever occurred before.

In her discussion of the two types of problems[11], University of Warwick professor Irene Ng gives makes the following comparison.

Complicated outcomes include:
1. getting the passenger's baggage from London to Sydney;
2. designing and constructing a town;
3. brain surgery;
4. putting a man on the moon.

---

10   I'm guided here by a paper by Dr. Sholom Glouberman and Dr. Brenda Zimmerman, entitled "Complicated and Complex Systems: What Would Successful Reform of Medicare Look Like?", Discussion Paper No. 8, Commission on the Future of Health Care in Canada, July 2002. Available at: http://publications.gc.ca/site/eng/235920/publication.html

11   "Complicated vs Complex Outcomes". http://value-basedservicesystem.blogspot.co.uk/2011/08/complicated-vs-complex-outcomes.html. 15 August 2011.

Examples of complex outcomes include:

1. giving the passenger a good experience flying from London to Sydney;
2. creating a community;
3. making a population healthy;
4. bringing up a child.

The outcomes we want in business and organisational life will fall on a spectrum, from simple, to complicated, to complex. But the big ones, the transformational ones, such as updating your business model, changing your culture, or capturing share in a new market, are likely to be complex.

What's working around here? Avoiding the trap of situational symmetry

As I said above, our reflex response to a problem or to a desired outcome is to sit down at the drawing board and design a solution that seems to equal the problem in terms of its scale and detail. But this is to take a complicated approach – linear, deterministic – to solve a complex problem. It is the trap of situational symmetry, and it won't work. On their own, our deterministic brains are not equal to the task of solving a complex problem.

"We have spent the last 100 years doing complicated rather well," wrote Irene Ng. "We can pat our backs [for] putting the man on the moon, doing brain surgeries etc. We are now moving to a world where complex outcomes matter and this is a new capability." Ng said we even need a new language: "We can **determine** complicated outcomes. We can only **enable** complex outcomes. We can **specify** complicated systems. We can only **intervene** in complex systems." (I've followed Ng's bolded emphases.)

Regarding child malnutrition in Vietnam, many smart people had asked the question: "What is the problem and how can we fix it?" A detailed answer to that question, provided, say, by expensive consultants, would waste reams of paper and be useless. An honest answer would be: "We don't know." With their Positive Deviance approach, the Sternins rejected that question and asked a very different one, namely: "What is working around here and how can we do more of it?" This is a profound mindset shift. Instead of imposing a solution from the outside they looked for the necessary wisdom and capability that was already there, latent, concealed among the villagers.

In delegation the trap of situational symmetry draws you as delegator into engineering a massive solution, or plan – think of it as a great big machine – and then handing responsibility for using and maintaining the great big machine over to the delegatee. Your job then becomes fretting and fussing over the delegatee's management of the great big machine, which amounts to micromanaging, and anyway will not solve the complex problem. Or you could instruct your delegatee to build their own great big machine according to your detailed specifications and then monitor them as they build it and try to use it, which also amounts to micromanaging, and still won't solve the complex problem. What you really want is for the delegatee to be, like Jerry and Monique Sternin, outposts of independent, dynamic capability. For that to work, you'll need a true letting go mindset: permit and empower them to seek out the wisdom and capacity hidden in the system and enable it to emerge as a solution.

What your delegatee looks for, specifically, will depend on your situation, but previously overlooked 'things that are working around here' could be:

1. relationships that produce good and surprising results;
2. useful skillsets you didn't know you had;
3. data or information you hadn't thought about what to do with;
4. an asset, like a building or a piece of intellectual property.

Progress versus perfection

Does this mean we should spend no time at all creating a plan to solve a problem or achieve a result? No. The Sternins had a plan. They didn't know exactly what they were looking for, but they were pretty sure it was there and they knew they'd know it when they found it. Furthermore, they had worked out where to look, how to look and, once they'd found it, they stopped and planned what to do about it. Plans get us started, but the lesson from Positive Deviance is that getting started on the journey is more important than wasting time on a detailed route map that will become obsolete when you hit the first fork in the road. So, your plan with the delegatee could sound something like this: "We want to achieve this and, having given it some thought, we think the way to do that is X, Y and Z, so we're going to get started right away, try those things, but keep our eyes and minds open along the way."

When I work with executive teams aiming for a big goal we peek up at the goal for orientation purposes but keep our focus firmly on the intermediate milestones directly ahead, and measure progress against where we started, not against how far we must go. (I'm grateful to Dan Sullivan for this insight.) Focussing on the gap between where we are and where we want to be can sap confidence and freeze us. (It is far more common than you might think for people to say: "I'd love to learn to play the piano, but if I can't play like Mozart in six months, what's the point?") Focussing on progress instead of perfection builds confidence, which boosts our energy, stimulates lateral thinking, and helps us take necessary risks. If you are constantly reminding your delegatee of how far from perfection their project is, and letting them know how much it bothers you, they will be less confident and less capable. But there is a balance to be struck, because praise for no good reason leads to complacency, delusion and error.

Let's move on. The point of deep and deliberate delegation is to seed and grow outposts of independent, dynamic capability, where great things are happening but it's not you doing them. But you will not abandon the delegatee; she needs stable feedback supply lines. Think of them as pipes through which flow a solution comprising the right amount of encouragement and direction. The discussion about how you set up those pipes and what you send through them takes us to the art of feedback.

Chapter 11 Reflections, ideas and tools

Reflection • Think of the Courageous outcome you want. Is it more difficult than the Sternins' challenge of solving child malnutrition in Vietnam?

Idea • An ambitious delegation is complex, not complicated, which means you cannot devise in advance a fool proof plan for achieving it. Like the Sternins' approach to tackling child malnutrition in Vietnam, you will need to really let go, and support the delegatee as he feels his way along, seeking the necessary wisdom and capability that is already there, latent and concealed in the systems.

Idea • Achieving complex outcomes requires us to avoid the trap of situational symmetry, meaning our urge, when faced with a complex problem, to try and design a solution that seems equal to the problem in terms of its scale and detail.

Tool • Harness the power of Positive Deviance: Do not ask "What is the problem and how can we fix it?" Instead, ask "What is working around here, and how can we do more of it?"

Tool • Value progress, and do not be paralysed by perfection: cultivate your confidence by focussing on the distance travelled from the beginning, not on the distance remaining to the end. (Thanks for the insight, Dan Sullivan!)

PART FOUR:
THE ART OF FEEDBACK

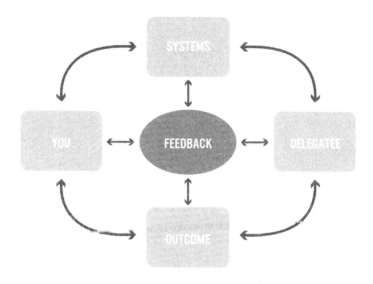

Overview

The act of delegation makes the delegatee accountable for calling into being a new, intended reality, and feedback is what nurtures the successful realisation of that accountability. In this section I argue that in organisational life today there is a widespread mishandling of both accountability and of feedback. Clear goals are often absent. When they are absent at the top of an organisation, this aimlessness seeps down through all of it. And yet companies still try and do what they think is feedback. That's why we have annual appraisals, because we cannot shake the feeling that we need to be helping employees 'improve'. This is also why so many people dislike the annual appraisal. It angers and alienates them because it is feedback without purpose.

Feedback is the 'pipe' through which flow the nutrients of encouragement, advice and challenge from delegator to delegatee, and back through which flow to the delegator essential intelligence about the endeavour. This requires a 'big' conversation, one that holds the delegatee to account, but in a way that builds mutual trust and confidence. Few of us emerge into working life fully equipped to give such feedback, and so a method for conducting the Delegation Feedback Conversation is proposed. Feedback cannot always be nice, however. If the endeavour is at all ambitious, as it should be, the delegatee will be put to the test and will need to be challenged to raise his game. Higher challenge must be balanced with higher support, however, so feedback requires the delegator to raise her game as well, showing extra skill, consideration and commitment.

CHAPTER 12
TRUE FEEDBACK NEEDS TRUE ACCOUNTABILITY

In 2000, a talented, ambitious thirty-something-year-old named David Bolchover entered the annals of corporate history by pulling off an impressive feat. For nearly a whole year, this MBA-holding, Russian-speaking junior executive managed to draw a handsome monthly paycheque from a large, London-headquartered insurance company without ever going into the office or troubling his repose with an ounce of work.

He didn't set out to deceive the company. On the contrary, his curious predicament arose after he had taken the initiative to make himself more valuable to it. In 1997 he'd landed his well-paid post selling insurance to Russian firms, but the job turned out to be extremely cushy. Left to his own devices, he would spend whole days doing little beyond making the occasional telephone call and chatting to the other well-qualified, under-deployed young men in his department. Bored and restless, he hatched a plan to enrol in a year-long MBA programme which, he reasoned, might pave the way to a more dynamic and engaging role in the firm. With this plan he went to one of his four bosses – the one he judged would be most receptive – and secured a generous agreement: the firm would pay half his tuition fees, a portion of his salary for living expenses, and would give him a full-time position, to be specified later, when he returned with his MBA in a year. Off he went to the halls of academe, and he emerged after a year with a renewed sense of energy, excitement and optimism.

However, even though he had been in touch, once, with his boss during the year and had, separately, explained his position to the HR department, when he returned he found that his boss had retired, and that no post had been found for him. All the same, as agreed, HR faithfully resumed paying his full salary. His case was briefly and half-heartedly taken up by a senior executive, and several meetings were arranged with other departments in the firm, but no new position materialised. Having fallen through a gaping organisational crack onto a big feather bed, he settled into a routine of reading, watching films, taking long walks and lunching with envious friends. Finally, ten months after being back on full pay, he was discovered by the division out of whose budget his salary was being drawn, and was called in to give an account of himself. There wasn't much to say. No doubt with embarrassment all round, he was made redundant – with a bountiful severance package, of course.

Bolchover used this story to set the scene for his book, *The Living Dead: Switched Off, Zoned Out, The Shocking Truth About Office Life* (Capstone, 2005), in which he argues that slacking off, fuelled by monumental employee disengagement, is rife in organisational life today. The effects of widespread, soul-destroying tedium and bad, absent management are luridly evident in statistics he offers up showing rampant in-work drug use, online time-wasting, and ballooning absenteeism. But the effects are most vividly distilled in his own, year-long internal holiday.

I'm not convinced that slacking off is as widespread now and everywhere as it was in the financial services sector in London before the crash of 2008. In the sector I grew up in, construction and engineering, with its razor-thin profit margins and disaster always ever only a hairsbreadth away, a 'Bolchover' would be spotted in an afternoon. But I agree with him that employee disengagement caused by boredom, aimlessness, and a sense of isolation and futility is widespread and terribly corrosive, both in sectors where people have too much time on their hands and where people are overworked and burning out.

The antidote to employee disengagement is deep and deliberate delegation, which assigns genuine, living account- ability, and which in turn is enabled by good feedback. The delegator assigns a stretching accountability for something to the delegatee, making her accountable for calling into being a new, intended reality. Feedback is what nurtures the successful reali- sation of that accountability. Through feedback, the delegatee is held to account, a phrase that evokes suspense because it implies being put to the test. And yes, feedback does involve that. But that is only part of it. Also through feedback, the delegatee receives the support and advice she needs to accomplish what she is supposed to accomplish, in order, eventually, to be able to account for herself favourably.

Based on my experience over many years as a senior manager, and for as many years again as a coach to companies, I believe that in organisational life today there is a widespread mishan- dling of both accountability as a concept, and of feedback as a tool for nurturing it. We get accountability wrong, and we get feedback wrong, and the two are intertwined.

How do we get accountability wrong? To explore that, I will put forward the idea that there is good accountability and bad accountability. Good accountability sets a person an obligation that is properly defined, is mutually agreed to, and is achievable, meaning the person has the freedom, authority and tools to do all the things necessary to meet the obligation. Here, we have re-entered the subjects of SMART and Courageous goal-setting (see Chapters 9 and 10). Good accountability is enabling and inspiring; the person is activated as an agent in bringing about a new, good reality, and is supported in that through feedback.

Accountability is bad, by which I mean meaningless or compromised, in three situations. It is bad, first, when it sets an obligation that is unrealistic or unachievable because the person does not have the freedom, authority or tools to meet the obligation. Second, accountability is bad if the obligation is not defined, or is poorly defined and open to competing inter-pretations. Under this circumstance, whether the person has met her obligations or not will be a matter of eternal dispute. Thirdly, accountability is bad if what the person is supposed to do is arbitrarily changed without the person's consent, or if the person's authority, freedom and tools are removed or tampered with. In common language this is called 'moving the goalposts'. In the realm of employment tribunals, it's called constructive dismissal. Under these three conditions there is no accounta-bility because the person is simply unable, by definition, to be held to account.

Many organisations I have come into contact with suffer in varying degrees from bad accountability. Clear goals are absent.

They are absent at the top of the organisation and this aimlessness seeps down through all of it. Bolchover does not explain
why his job was so boring: whether, for instance, his department's
sales targets were negligibly low, or were perhaps entirely absent,
or were never checked by anyone above. In any event, it appears
that he was accountable for nothing. Companies may think they
have goals because they have headline financial targets, but these
are the weakest, most basic, default-setting sort of goals. You can
come up with a good-looking number that represents desired
turnover, profit, debt level or share price, but that number has
nothing to say about how you're going to achieve the target,
or what sort of company you're going to be. Left to their own
devices, company departments will supply default-setting goals
of their own that support the headline financial targets but,
again, these say nothing about how to get there or what sort of
department or team they will be. At the individual level, with
their organisation denuded of inspiration or direction, people
make do with performing routine functions, being cogs and
doing their bit to keep the organisation ticking over.

With good accountability, feedback has a purpose, and its
effectiveness can be seen and felt in the demonstrable progress
toward the goal. Under bad accountability feedback has no
purpose, because there is no goal. Feedback here becomes
random: an arbitrary reprimand or a reassuring little chat.
Companies still try and 'do' feedback because employees can
always improve and because, without checks and monitoring,
organisations will drift into disorder and decline. Off-the-shelf
annual appraisals give the illusion of feedback for companies that
lack clear organisational goals, which is why people dislike the

annual appraisal. It angers and alienates them precisely because it is feedback applied to situations of bad accountability; it is feedback without real purpose.

Survey data amply demonstrate the unpopularity and even the ineffectiveness of annual performance appraisals. Trashing this yearly ritual is something of a mini industry, in fact. To quote a recent example, in their international 2016 study, compensation consultants Willis Towers Watson found that fewer than half (48%) of employees report that performance reviews have helped improve their performance, while only 52% believe their performance was accurately evaluated in their most recent review. My own experience, comprising ten years on the receiving end of these reviews, ten years on the giving end, and twenty more witnessing their effect as a coach, has cemented my dislike for them. Here, typically, is what happens. You go in to meet your boss. You haven't done any preparation and neither, probably, has he. You are asked a set of questions about what you think you are good at, what you think you are bad at, what you are proud of over the year, what you are ashamed of, what you see as your priorities or objectives for the coming year, what will hinder meeting those, and what the company could do to help. ("Not that we're making any promises, mind you.")

Then the boss serves what is known as the 'feedback sandwich', which consists of some praise for what you're good at, some criticism of what you're bad at, followed by some reparative praise for more random things you're good at. The idea here is that the praise makes the criticism easier to swallow, but what happens is very different. When it comes, the first serving of praise feels false and obligatory, the criticism makes me feel angry and defensive, and I don't even hear the second serving of praise because I'm stewing about the criticism. There follows a superficial conversation about the training or 'support' I need to help me get better at what I'm bad at, and we part, me feeling angry and defensive, the boss also feeling uncomfortable. Then, with relief, all is forgotten for a year until the dismal exercise is due to be repeated.

There are two big things wrong with this approach. The first is that in an aimless team or organisation, where a specific, mutually recognised accountability is not there to assess, the off-the-shelf appraisal imposes a template for an idealised employee with a checklist of traits and behaviours that may not have any relevance to the employee's real job or circumstances. And against this idealised template the boss must find fault because nobody is ideal and not to find fault would be to subvert the appraisal's underlying assumption, which is that everyone can, and should, improve. It is the imposition of an alien bureaucratic procedure onto the employee's *ad hoc* system of obligations, stresses and relationships that, however weak and aimless, is nevertheless real. The result is that I go into an appraisal knowing I'm going to be asked meaningless questions, which only accentuates the underlying aimlessness of my working life, and tense in the knowledge that I'm about to be criticised for no good reason. To prepare, I think up some suitably non-incriminating things to say in response to the questions, and brace myself for the feedback sandwich.

Secondly, this approach focuses, however slyly, on a person's weaknesses, and takes their strengths as givens. The terrible futility of this is that I could spend an entire career improving my weaknesses and all I would end up with is stronger weaknesses: in other words, mediocrity. To use a provocative example, it would be like the coach of tennis champion Andy Murray, in the run up to the US Open, diverting precious coaching time to raise the issue of Murray's untidy approach to his kit, and the need to show more empathy in his dealings with one of the junior coaching or admin staff. Some HR practitioners may see this as unfair, but for employees marooned in situations of bad accountability, it is how the annual appraisal can feel.

By no means is the antidote to bad annual appraisals merely to leave people alone. We want mastery and autonomy, as Daniel Pink argues, but that doesn't mean splendid isolation. We need help, guidance and a sense of connection. We want to grow the value of our contribution to the whole. We want to matter, and our immediate manager can make sure we do, and feel that we do. A 2015 study by Gallup revealed that managers account for up to 70% of variance in employee engagement and, further, that employees whose managers hold regular meetings with them are almost three times as likely to be engaged as employees whose managers do not.[12]

Leading companies are catching on. IBM, GE, Adobe, Microsoft and others are moving away from annual appraisals toward more frequent, and more explicitly goal-oriented,

---

12   Jim Harter and Amy Adkins, "Employees Want a Lot More From Their Managers", Gallup Business Journal, April 8, 2015. Online at: http://www. gallup.com/businessjournal/182321/employees-lot-managers.aspx

feedback techniques.[13] This is a good sign, and overdue, but in some instances the changes still appear to pursue feedback as an end in itself, as something that can be nurtured whether conditions of genuine accountability exist or not. It can't. Accountability comes first, and is actuated by feedback.

In any case, you do not need to wait for a top-down organisational change programme to roll through town before you start injecting into your team genuine accountability supported by effective feedback, with all the excitement and buy-in this engenders. You can just start. Deep and deliberate delegation is the *guerrilla*-style, ground-up restoration of purpose and engagement in work, of the sort that would have made David Bolchover a star in his company.

Through feedback the delegatee is held to account but is also assisted through encouragement and guidance. This kind of robust feedback connects you and the delegatee, but it requires something rare: an ability to hold an awkward but productive conversation, one which ensures both parties get what they need in order to progress the delegation, including accurate information for you and, sometimes, corrective challenges for the delegatee. Such a conversation is a big conversation, and in the next chapter we explore why they are necessary in delegation feedback.

---

13   Zillman, Claire, "IBM Is Blowing Up Its Annual Performance Review", *Fortune*, 1 February 2016. Online at: http://fortune.com/2016/02/01/ibm-employee-performance-reviews/

Chapter 12 Reflections, ideas and tools

Reflection • If you had to hold three awkward but productive conversations tomorrow, who would they be with, and what would they be about? Would you be equipped to hold them?

Idea • Without effective goal-setting there can be no holding to account and, therefore, no accountability. If there is no accountability, feedback is meaningless. It will lack purpose and be arbitrary. At worst, it is the mere projection onto an employee of the boss's own issues. So, deal with goal-setting and accountability first.

Idea • Where there is no true accountability, off-the-shelf annual appraisals anger and alienate employees because they impose a template for an idealised employee with a checklist of traits, competencies and behaviours that may have no relevance to the employee or her actual job.

Tool • Try forgetting about a person's weaknesses and instead praise and deploy their strengths. Improving weaknesses only leads to stronger weaknesses: in other words, mediocrity.

Idea • Deep and deliberate delegation bestows genuine accountability. As such, it is the ground-up restoration of purpose and engagement in work.

CHAPTER 13
SETTING THE SCENE FOR BIG CONVERSATIONS

It is a bright, clear morning, and you are standing on a ridge with your delegatee, slightly out of breath from the climb, looking up at the goal you want to reach. It is the peak, glittering in the early sunshine, of a tall mountain that rises up at the far end of a long valley that is densely forested and shrouded in mist. Down on the plain behind you from where you've just come is your field headquarters, a cluster of tents and temporary structures laid neatly out on the plain, around which already you can see people moving about, busy as ants.

This is an important day. It has been decided that your delegatee – let's call her Beth – will attempt to establish a camp up there on that peak. As mission leader you are the delegator and after careful consideration and discussions you chose Beth. This hasn't been easy for you. Until now it has been you who climbed the mountains and established camps. You climbed the first and for a long time it was generally accepted that no one could climb mountains as well as you. But as your mission has grown so too have your responsibilities and if you climb this mountain other important things will not get done. Just as important, if you climb this mountain and establish the camp the opportunity for up-and-coming talent in the mission to prove themselves will have been missed, again.

You and Beth exchange a glance. She has never climbed a mountain this tall on her own and has never established a camp. But then again neither had you when you climbed your first mountain and established your first camp. She has the skills to do most of the things she'll need to do and is smart enough to learn as she goes. And judging by the big smile on her face, she really wants this.

The reassuring look in her eyes also tells you she knows what you're thinking, which is: Are we really ready? Have we thought of every contingency? From an old map, the only one available, we know a river runs through the valley. There are ravines. The path is unmarked in places. But you've been through all this before. There are reports of a bridge across the river, somewhere, and anyway, rivers can be crossed. Ravines can be traversed. She has a compass and there are people in the valley who can help. The mountain is high and the summit is hard to reach but Beth has training and experience and, furthermore, you have it on good authority that there is a settlement of helpful guides at the mountain's base.

Two days ago you had a crisis of confidence. Everything that could go wrong – bad weather, faulty information, a failure of Beth's equipment, the possibility of her encountering something too difficult – reared up vividly in your mind. Wouldn't it be easier, quicker, simpler, you thought, if I just did this last one myself? Mixed in with those feelings was a pang of desire to hang on to the mountain-climbing glory and to enjoy once again the exhilaration of the ascent. But those feelings passed. You're sure again that this is the right thing and that she'll succeed.

Plus, you will be in regular contact by phone. A detailed and comprehensive plan is impossible but you've agreed on what the likely milestones will be and what success will look like as each of the milestones are reached, and the two of you can work things out as she proceeds.

Some last-minute meddling cannot be resisted, however.

"You see down there where the trees thin out into meadow? Just to the left of that hollow? I think that's where you pick up the path through the forest," you say.

"Yes, I know," Beth says. "We talked about that."

"And don't forget, when you see somebody make sure you speak to them and find out everything you can about the state of the path, and also whether there's a bridge."

"Of course I won't forget."

"And if you pass a spring or a brook fill up your spare bottles with water because you don't know when you'll be able to next."

"Yes, we talked about that, too."

Okay. It's time.

"Right then!" you say. "You've got your tent, your equipment, your supplies. Off you go. Call me tomorrow and let me know how you're getting on."

And off she goes, picking her way down the steep rocky path, looking up now and again with an excited smile. Then, suddenly, she slips on a gravelly patch and lurches horribly. But she recovers her footing, adjusts her pack, and gives a jaunty wave. A peal of embarrassed laughter wafts up. As you stand watching she gets smaller and smaller until a twist in the path takes her out of sight. You sigh. You're full of anticipation, too. Glory for the mission is in store. You're a little nervous but you know she can do this and things will be clearer tomorrow. You turn and head back down the other side of the ridge to headquarters where other pressing matters await.

Beth is activated. It is an exciting juncture for the delegation project: she's 'in the field'. But it doesn't mean you can go back to your desk and forget about her. She may be on the sharp end of the endeavour – and you register some relief at this as your joints complain on the jarring descent off the ridge – but much will be required of you, too, and it will take effort, commitment and a willingness to learn.

With delegation you give up the hard control that comes from originating and carrying out new initiatives all on your own. Hard control rightly gives way to something subtler: influence. But don't underestimate the power of influence. Remember, Beth still needs you. She needs advice and encouragement in order to have confidence and make good decisions in the field. She will also need to be challenged and corrected from time to time, as none of us are infallible. All this is feedback.

Feedback needs a medium – a pipe – and that medium is conversation. But it can't be just any old conversation, a bit of a chit-chat, an occasional word in the ear. The Delegation Feedback Conversation has a job to do. For it to be of service to the delegation project it must cover all the bases by allowing the following things to happen:

1. The delegatee gives an accurate report on progress made in reaching agreed milestones.
2. An assessment is made of the success or not of that progress.

3. Barriers to success are explored.
4. Strategies for overcoming those barriers are adopted.
5. Ways you can help are identified.
6. The delegatee is challenged where, however inadvertently, she is working against the aims of the project.
7. Milestones are reassessed, with some kept, others dropped, and new ones agreed as necessary.
8. She departs with new ideas, heightened clarity, and refreshed confidence and energy.
9. So do you.

This is a big conversation, of a sort we rarely have in organisational life today. The delegatee is being held to account but in a way that builds mutual trust and confidence, as opposed to eroding them. Feedback of this kind cannot be a once-in-a-job conversation, or even a once-a-year conversation: it must be held often, at regular intervals and between intervals if necessary, until the end goal is reached.

Few of us emerge into working life fully equipped to hold such a conversation. Some people are naturals, combining emotional fluency, perceptiveness (they can spot the right thing to say), verbal dexterity (they can improvise on the spot to say it), self-control, courage, and everything else that comes under the diplomatic skills umbrella. But there are not enough of these people to meet the demand for productive, difficult conversations in organisational life. We all have a conversational style developed from birth in accordance with our personality to help us cope and get along in life and work, with greater or lesser success. Some of us talk too much and never listen, while others retreat habitually into listening mode and offer up their thoughts only under duress. Some use speech primarily to criticise, challenge and demand, while others can bring themselves only to soothe and praise. Some overuse humour and others are tediously earnest. These are extremes, but my contention is that few of us are naturally equipped with a conversational style that does everything it needs to do adequately and reliably to foster bi-directional feedback between two people, especially if those two people barely know each other, and come from different work backgrounds and even cultures. Few managers receive training in this and default approved methods such as the feedback sandwich, as discussed in the previous chapter, can be inadequate.

Lacking techniques and strategies for holding big conversations, which can become difficult and which require honesty, commitment, and the breaching of comfort zones, managers often let friction fester until anger boils over. We come up with ways of appearing to carry on while avoiding confrontation, hoping that tensions will naturally subside, as the swelling when you bump your head does, until it becomes next to impossible to get around the room for the size of the elephant in it, which of course we don't mention. "Oh, we don't hold people to account, we just grumble," as a manager admitted to me quite readily, with a rueful chuckle. One managing director put it to me even more bluntly: "Nowadays poor performance is vastly time-consuming and the process of performance management is very stressful for the manager, so they ignore it. In fact, avoiding the stress and time involved has become an explicit objective for management." As a coach I'm familiar with organisational dysfunction but even I found this bleakly shocking. In such circumstances delegation can never happen. No wonder the same managing director also said to me: "People initially try to delegate something and nothing happens, and there is no consequence. They try again and nothing happens and there is still no consequence. So, the delegator just does it himself."

Since most of us receive exactly no training in how to conduct big conversations, which involve provoking a measure of discomfort while building, not eroding, mutual confidence and trust, I present in the next chapter a step-by-step method you can follow for holding the Delegation Feedback Conversation.

Chapter 13 Reflections, ideas and tools

Reflection • Think about your own conversational style. In what ways might it get in the way of holding productive conversations?

Idea • With delegation you give up hard control and replace it with something subtler: influence. But don't underestimate the power of influence. The delegatee still needs you. She needs advice and encouragement in order to have confidence and make good decisions in the field. She will also need to be challenged and corrected from time to time, because none of us are infallible. This is feedback.

Idea • Feedback needs a medium – a pipe – and that medium is conversation. The Delegation Feedback Conversation needs to be big because it has important jobs to do. In it, progress is reported and assessed, barriers are identified, strategies are devised, the delegatee is encouraged and challenged, and the delegator commits to help.

Idea • Few of us emerge into working life naturally equipped to hold such a conversation.

CHAPTER 14
HOW TO CONDUCT A DELEGATION FEEDBACK CONVERSATION

We need a technique for holding big conversations because few of us are born with one, and few of us are given the necessary training. So I am proposing here a simple method for holding the Delegation Feedback Conversation (or the Feedback Conversation). It is designed to help you and the delegatee cover everything. It gives everybody a speaking part and a framework for the necessary mix of inquiry, support, tactical planning and challenge. It loosens the tongues of the reticent, and constrains the loquacious and overbearing to keep their ears open and their mouths closed. It is a lean and flexible technique, capable of repetition anywhere, under almost any circumstance where a face-to-face conversation can be held. (And for reasons I will explain later it must be face to face. Video conference will just about do if absolutely necessary. Never by email or text.) It can be stretched out for an hour or packed into a few minutes. All you need is a comfortable, quiet space free of distraction and, ideally, a white board or sheets of paper.

The Feedback Conversation helps us move toward the end goal through a series of milestones. When Beth started off down the ridge she was heading not just physically for the forest but also toward a number of milestones you both agreed were important for early traction, picking up the trail, getting water and so on. In the real world, to which we now turn, these milestones could include any number of things Beth must accomplish, including procuring services, obtaining permissions, getting stakeholders on board, or discovering facts. To get started there should be no more than five, judged as the most critical for this stage of the project. Milestones are changeable and have limited shelf lives because as uncharted territory becomes charted they will be reached, or they will be discarded in favour of more relevant ones, and new ones will be adopted, all according to how the landscape is changing.

So, once Beth is activated, here is how it works.

Step 1. Score progress

After preliminaries that relax and focus you both, you review the milestones previously set. As mentioned before, there should be no more than five.

Then you pick the most important one and talk about it for a bit, reminding both of you why it was picked and what some of the anticipated difficulties were. Thus, warmed up to the topic, you invite Beth to rate progress on achieving that milestone by giving it a score of zero to ten. Beth thinks about it and supplies a score: four, say.

Then you ask: "Okay, what is the primary reason for your score?" This sparks a conversation, where Beth explains the primary reason and you mostly listen, speaking only to ask questions for the purpose of clarity. Make notes on the reason.

Then you ask a second prompting question: "What would

need to have happened for you to score a ten?" This sparks the second phase of discussion, in which Beth talks about why the score is not ten. Again, you do more listening than talking at this stage.

This process is repeated for each of the milestones, resulting in five scores, which can be written on the white board. You and Beth add up these five scores, and divide them by five, to get an average. Let's say it is 4.7. This average is Beth's Happy Score. You will keep track of this Happy Score in Feedback Conversations throughout the delegation because if it is trending upward that means progress is being made, and if it is not moving or is trending downward, something is wrong.

Step 2. Reset the milestones

In this part, you and Beth agree on a new set of milestones. You invite Beth to consider the ultimate goal, the outcome of the delegation, and to name the top five things that must happen before the next Feedback Conversation in order to meet that objective in the given time. Remember that here we are in territory that is now at least partially charted, though is perhaps not conquered. Depending on what was discussed, these new milestones could be previous ones repeated (because they are still critical, and new approaches have been identified in reaching them); in between ones that are stepping stones to the former ones; or, encouragingly, entirely new ones set out beyond charted territory. In this part of the conversation you have a more active role, offering advice and information, challenging and encouraging Beth, and agreeing to provide specific assistance. With these new milestones, and armed with new ideas and refreshed confidence and energy, Beth heads back out into the field. You, meanwhile, prepare to provide the assistance promised. Here is a visual representation of the Feedback Conversation cycle.

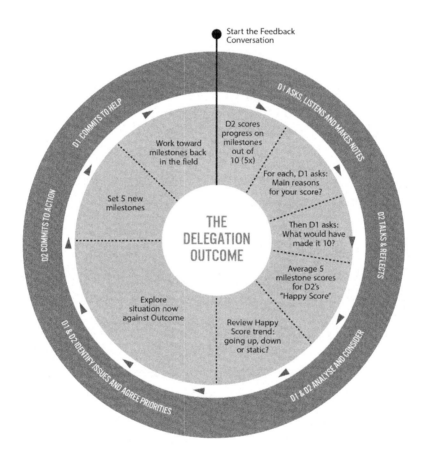

FIGURE 3. The Delegation Feedback Conversation Cycle, where D1 is the delegator, and D2 is the delegatee (Credit: Dave Stitt)

There are variations you can apply to Step 2, which I'll discuss next, but first I'd like to say a few things about this basic technique. There are three main reasons why I like it.

First, I like it because it is light, quick and participatory.

Second, I like it because it puts Beth in the driver's seat. I stole the milestone progress scoring method from a powerful customer feedback tool called the Net Promoter Score, which asks customers to score the service they received from zero to ten, and asks the two follow-up questions given above: "What's the primary reason for your score?" and "What needs to happen for it to be ten?" This trusts the customer to know their mind, and asks them to pick the main thing that went wrong. It doesn't try and catch them out with tricky, contra-indicating questions. It asks merely, "What do you think, and why?" Similarly, the Feedback Conversation trusts Beth to know what is going on, to know what the main barrier to progress is, and to think up ways of overcoming it. This has the effect of keeping you at a precise distance, of preventing you from moving in and retaking ownership of the delegation with an exhaustive analysis and a detailed, prescriptive plan.

Third, by focussing more on Beth's Happy Score than on the milestones, the Feedback Conversation encourages tactical flexibility. Let's remember that strategy is the big, overall plan while tactics are the mini-judgements you make 'on the hoof' to realise it. Beth orients herself by glancing up at the ultimate goal (strategy), and then considers the territory she is in and resets the milestones (tactics) accordingly. To insist that every stated milestone be fully achieved before moving on to the next is to seek comfort in tactical success at the possible expense of strategic success.

Now we will explore two variations on Step 2 of the Feedback Conversation that can help when Beth is 1) emotionally paralysed, and 2) in danger of giving up.

Reset the milestones, Variation 1: Overcoming emotional paralysis with DOS

In Step 2 above you simply ask Beth to pick five new (or repeat) milestones. This is fine when things are going smoothly, when there is a good flow of communication between the two of you, when progress is palpable and there is plenty of confidence. There are two situations, however, when this step requires more considered handling. One is when negative emotions are running high, when Beth is feeling stress, worry, or anger because she is overwhelmed or has suffered setbacks, and feedback from her is laced with panic and lament. Here the Feedback Conversation must recognise those emotions so that the edge can be taken off them, allowing Beth to see more clearly and regain confidence. The other can be the flip-side of the same coin, when Beth seems flat, detached and withdrawn, and feedback from her is not real, in that it is full of evasions, generalities and clichés. This is usually a sign that she is unhappy with progress, and is managing her negative emotions by keeping a lid on them. She wants to prevent you from getting too near to protect her equilibrium and buy time. (We'll examine this more in the next chapter.)

Beth's feelings and privacy must be respected but if this situation persists over several Feedback Conversations her feelings are getting in the way, creating a blockage in the feedback 'pipe'. This will undermine the delegation, so she must be helped to open up so that, again, negative emotions lose their power and confidence and clarity can be restored.

The variation I'm suggesting here is drawn from a technique developed by the coach of entrepreneurs, Dan Sullivan, known as the DOS Conversation, where DOS stands for dangers, opportunities and strengths. To bring this into play you ask Beth to name the top three things she is afraid of, or worried about (dangers), and these are written on the white board. Then you ask her to name the top three things she is excited about (opportunities), also to be recorded on the white board. In the same way, you ask Beth to name the top three things she needs in order to feel confident about this phase of the delegation (strengths). So, on the white board now are nine items – three dangers, three opportunities and three (potential) strengths. After allowing a moment for reflection you press further, asking Beth to pick from the nine items just five that matter most right now to the delegation. Having selected these as the five biggest issues for the delegation right now, you ask Beth to identify, for each big issue, what needs to happen in order for her to feel happy with progress at the next Feedback Conversation. These are recorded and agreed as the next five milestones.

The DOS Conversation can help ease Beth off the fence by requesting more detailed and specific feedback. You can politely resist any attempt by her to retreat into generality by asking "What do you mean by that?" or "What would that look like?" It also recognises and brings out into the open the strongest and most paralysing emotion, fear, and defangs it by naming and delineating the risks. A risk delineated is a risk with its limits defined, leaving space outside those limits for a response. This approach also taps into the strong emotions of excitement and confidence, which help us think more clearly and more creatively, and which fuel robust responses to risk, propelling us out of paralysis and into action.

Reset the milestones, Variation 2: Facing brutal facts with the Stockdale Paradox

This variation can help when Beth is paralysed not by fear but by despair, when she has concluded that the delegation is hopeless, that the barriers are simply too great for her to overcome. The Stockdale Paradox refers to the inadequacy of both optimism and pessimism in the face of unimaginable hardship. It was named by author Jim Collins in his book, *Good to great: Why some companies make the leap ... and others don't* (HarperBusiness, 2001), in which he records an interview with the American pilot Jim Stockdale who was shot down over North Vietnam in 1965 and held prisoner for seven years and five months. Beaten, tortured and kept in a tiny, windowless cell, Stockdale survived when other US captives died. By his account, pessimists lost hope and died from a broken heart. For their part, optimists would try and keep their hopes alive by telling themselves that their ordeal would end, say, by Christmas and when it didn't that it would end by the summer, and so on. These, too, died of a broken heart. Stockdale's response was not pessimistic, since he never lost faith that eventually he would prevail, and that this ordeal would be the defining event of his life. But he also forced himself to confront and accept the reality of the most brutal facts of his situation without allowing himself the anaesthetic of false hope.

Your delegation project is trivial compared to Stockdale's ordeal, but we can use the lessons from it without trivialising it. The paradox demonstrates something important, which is that brutal facts may be brutal and real, but how we respond to them is up to us. We can give up or we can cling on to faith that we will prevail in the end and keep trying; in other words, show grit.

You can help Beth discover her grit in this variation by inviting her to name the five most brutal facts of the situation, which are the biggest barriers to progress. She articulates them and up they go on the white board. With the brutal facts thus named, defined and delineated, space opens up around their borders, allowing the possibility of a response. You focus on this space by going through each brutal fact and asking Beth to identify one thing that needs to happen in order for her to be happier with her progress at the next Feedback Conversation. This one thing might tackle the brutal fact head on and dismantle it, or seek to contain it and limit its impact, or even just work around it. The thing might be an action on Beth's part, or it might involve assistance from you. Out of this process come the next five milestones.

This set of instructions for holding a Feedback Conversation may seem overly prescriptive, and following them may feel unnatural for you both at first. But I have dared to be prescriptive because the Feedback Conversation has a big job to do and we are not used to holding these sorts of conversations. That big job is to score progress against milestones and to set new milestones, allowing the regular and frequent replenishment of clarity and confidence. Over time, you both may find you are having that conversation in a more natural and condensed way and that the deliberate steps of the Feedback Conversation feel clunky and procedural. If that is the case, feel free to drop them.

How frequently the Feedback Conversation is held will depend on the length of time involved in the delegation and the velocity and impact of the change it is bringing about. Once a month seems reasonable in a multi-month delegation project while once a week may suit if the delegation project enters a "white water" patch and a greater volume of feedback is needed to keep it on track.

I said earlier that the Feedback Conversation must be face to face, or by video conference if necessary. I say this because in organisations today, electronic communications are steadily stealing territory from face-to-face interactions. Partly this is because organisations are more physically distributed. Partly, too, it's because email is easier, quicker, and does away with all that time-consuming and messy interpersonal stuff. But this takeover has gone too far, with email now being used for interactions that should only happen face to face. If the conversation is in any sense big, meaning there needs to be mutual understanding, negotiation and commitment, email will not do. It wastes time and leads to misunderstandings that can escalate into conflict quite unnecessarily. Here is what happens. With email, we think we're communicating, but really we're just transmitting words. Albert Mehrabian, a pioneer on the understanding of communications since the 1960s, found that, in the communication of feelings and attitudes:

- only 7% of the spoken message is received through the words themselves;
- 38% of the message comes through the tone of voice; and
- 55% of the message comes through body language, mostly from eye contact.

Email, which deals in words only, is a weak, low-bandwidth medium when it comes to conveying feelings and attitudes, and it matters because, when you have to talk about something difficult, the other person needs to see and hear your words coming out, and you need to see and hear your words going in. They can see 'where you're coming from', that is, sense your attitudes and feelings. They can understand your perspective and empathise. They can also ask questions to clarify what's required of them, and ask for assistance or for things in return – in other words, negotiate. When you are face-to-face, assurances can be given, bargains made, and confidence instilled all in minutes with the help of looks, gestures, demeanour and tone of voice. Hammering it out by email would take hours, days even, and still leave lots of room to wriggle or for grave misunderstandings. People can tell themselves that, having crafted and sent a long email, they have 'got their point across', that they have 'set things straight' and that if the recipient doesn't get it then it is their problem and there is nothing more to be done. This is not the case at all and is why endeavours fail. Email is fine for simple transactions and informing people of things but for something as important as the Feedback Conversation you need the high bandwidth of face to face.

This leads us to the topic of difficult conversations. While the Feedback Conversation is a good framework to guide a big, working conversation its mechanisms are not robust enough always to guarantee success. In laying out the method I've emphasised the supportive role of the delegator, with the assumption that the delegatee will always be open and receptive. In the real world, however, tensions will arise and sometimes you have to get tough.

Chapter 14 Reflections, ideas and tools

Tool • The Delegation Feedback Conversation

1. Pick the five most important milestones needed to move the delegation forward right now.
2. The delegatee rates progress on the first milestone with a score of zero to ten.
3. Ask her, "What is the main reason for your score?" Listen, make notes.
4. Then ask her, "What would need to have happened for you to score a ten?" Listen and make notes.
5. When all five milestones have been scored and discussed, average the scores to get the delegatee's Happy Score. Record this to track progress.
6. Review notes and reset the milestones, five new ones, to be scored at the next Feedback Conversation.
7. Encourage the delegatee, and agree on how you will help with the new milestones.

Tool • The DOS conversation: If the delegatee is paralysed by emotion, reset the milestones by holding a DOS conversation, exploring dangers, opportunities and strengths.

Tool • The Stockdale Paradox: If morale is really suffering, reset milestones by facing brutal facts.

CHAPTER 15
WHEN, AND HOW, TO GET TOUGH

We assume our delegatee is broadly equipped to perform the delegation and will not lie or knowingly sabotage it. Consider the resourceful Beth, no longer in the metaphorical forest, but in the real world. We don't doubt her trustworthiness but she is human, and so are you. Tensions will always arise because nobody is perfect. Even when we are honourable, committed and talented, we are fallible. The best of us make errors of judgement, suffer lapses of attention and experience slumps in energy and motivation. Our self-awareness is imperfect and we are sometimes prone to taking shortcuts. Periodically we become pig-headed or too snug in our comfort zones. Situations will arise in the delegation in which you need to challenge the delegatee, including when she:

1. seems committed to a course of action that you think won't work;
2. gets embroiled in conflict with someone whose cooperation is needed;
3. is stuck, has stopped making progress, has become demotivated and evasive, is suffering from enthusiasm half-life;

4. is overwhelmed by all she must do, of which this delegation is only a part.

We thrive with support, but we also thrive on challenge. Skilful managers, and skilful delegators, cultivate a mindset that balances the two. Consider the Support-Challenge Matrix, developed by coaches John Blakey and Ian Day in their book, *Challenging Coaching*, which provides an extremely useful visualisation of the dynamic at play.

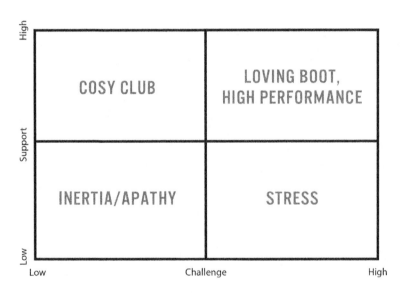

FIGURE 4. The Support Challenge Matrix (Credit: John Blakey and Ian Day)

What it shows is that if I am providing little support and little challenge, my people are in the zone of inertia, apathy, isolation and boredom. I don't care much, and neither will they. I am not committed and engaged, and they aren't either. They're showing up, going through the motions, and collecting their pay.

If I am providing low levels of support but high levels of challenge ("You did it wrong!" "If you can't do this I'll find someone who can!") my people will experience mostly stress, which is debilitating. This is the zone of low morale, blame, risk aversion and uneven performance. Placed in this zone for too long, people burn out or jump ship.

Swinging over to the top-left quadrant if I am providing lots of support but no challenge I am coddling my people. This is the zone of smug complacency (Cosy Club is the term Blakey and Day coined), characterised by low standards, low achievement, a sense of entitlement, and stasis. Champion athletes who stray into the Cosy Club will lose their titles, and businesses their customers. If, however, I get the balance right by providing high levels of challenge and high levels of support, my people move into the Loving Boot quadrant. This is the sweet spot, the zone of excitement, high performance and consistently good results, often better than any of us might have expected.

The nature or size of the delegation project determines the required levels of support and challenge. If it is a one-off task it will require limited challenge and limited support from me. If it is a Courageous outcome then I and the delegatee will both have to raise our games. She will have to draw more heavily on her intellectual and emotional resources, and I will have to supply bigger support and challenge and be more considered and deft in getting the balance right. Let's see how the Support-Challenge Matrix might applied to the four scenarios above with you and Beth.

She seems committed to a course of action you think won't work

Even when two people are deeply committed to a goal, conflict can arise over how to achieve it, especially if you've granted the delegatee some autonomy. Let's say Beth is working on assumptions that seem unsound to you and you believe there is a risk of unnecessary difficulties if she carries on. If you were in the Zone of Apathy you might shrug your shoulders and say, "Well, I guess we'll see how it goes, then, won't we?" But this is important, and you care. So, you explain your reservations as best you can (you may not be entirely clear on them yourself just yet). But Beth isn't listening so, in a sudden failure of patience, you crank up the challenge dial and launch into the Zone of Stress. "Beth," you say abruptly, "your course of action isn't working. I've given you my reasons, now I want you to re-think your approach. Come back in the morning and tell me what you've come up with."

Next morning, Beth looks tired and unhappy. She's rattled and the milestones she proposes are muddled. Suddenly unsure of yourself and worried at the stress you've caused, you crank the support dial up into the Cosy Club. "Good work, Beth," you say. "Some great ideas there and you've been hard at it. I tell you what. This is all a bit tricky, isn't it? How about you leave it with me and I'll think it through and give you my thoughts in a few days?" And off Beth goes, suspended from the delegation. You've assumed her burden and disempowered her: lose-lose.

Realising your mistake, the next day you schedule a meeting and try again, this time having a go at working both dials at once. You acknowledge that Beth has confidence in her original approach but point out that your reservations can't just be ignored. Having had time to gather your thoughts you explain in more detail what you think might go wrong. Then you accept her lead in setting the milestones but for a nearer horizon, and with the next Feedback Conversation scheduled a week hence. Beth is happy with that, so you ease up the challenge dial some more by asking for a discussion of ways her plan might be made more flexible in order to handle the difficulties you foresee, but whose likelihood the two of you disagree on. This chafes a bit for Beth but after a few minutes some contingency strategies are drawn up and the two of you part, each of you having upped your game and with accountability and honour intact.

In this scenario I've had you veer into the Zone of Stress, and then up over into the Cosy Club, because that is normal. It is not realistic to expect that every bit of feedback you give can be perfectly calibrated on the Support-Challenge Matrix. Sometimes a bit of anger and stress are called for and sometimes we all need to be coddled. Feedback is an art, not a science, requiring practice and the development of knack.

She gets embroiled in a conflict with someone whose cooperation is needed

This is a difficult one, but I would not want to get pulled into the conflict, for instance by weighing in on Beth's side, or by mediating directly between her and the other person, or by going over their heads to the other person's boss to impose a resolution. Fighting Beth's battles for her is Cosy Club. We have to deal with people if we are to achieve anything out of the ordinary, and Beth will never succeed in the delegation if she cannot navigate her way through the growing web of relationships the delegation will spin. However, something is required of me if I am not merely to be apathetic and duck the issue with, "Yeah, people are so unreasonable. Bummer." I could turn up the support by giving her the opportunity to vent and tell her side of the story, but I would also turn up the challenge by encouraging her to examine her own part in conflict. To employ a coaching technique, sometimes a simple role play that explores what led to the standoff can unlock perceptions into how to resolve it. I may have advice to offer, which, if done right, is both support-ive and challenging. I might edge the challenge up further by asking Beth how she can modify her approach in order to move things forward whatever the rights and wrongs of the matter. A stress-inducing response would be to lay the blame at her feet and say, "Come back to me when it's sorted." Sometimes that might be what is needed.

She is stuck, has stopped making progress, and has become demotivated and evasive

If despondency stretches out over several Feedback Conversa-tions – even after you've tried the DOS Conversation and the Stockdale Paradox – and you sense that the scoring and renewing of milestones has lost meaning for Beth, you will need to find out what's going on. Brace yourself, though. She may be having a personal crisis or is about to leave for another job, or it may be that something about your approach is causing her problems. The sooner you know, the sooner something can be done about it. A negligent approach, one that is common in organisational life, would be for me to bury myself in my own work and assume she will eventually snap out of it, and even to conclude that if she doesn't then the failure of the endeavour will be her fault, not mine. This is a poor attitude. It means I am happy to see the endeavour founder as long the tranquillity of my own comfort zone is not disturbed.

Beth's evasiveness is the key issue here because it means the feedback pipe is blocked. It is best to address it politely but directly. A challenging opener would be: "It feels to me that things have gone flat around here, Beth. You seem distant and disengaged. What's going on?"

If she is in evasive mode she may counter-challenge with, "Really? What makes you say that?", and you must have specifics to hand, for example, "Well, you were going to deliver x and y by last week, and you didn't, and you haven't said anything about it, which is unusual for you, so naturally I'm concerned."

This puts Beth on the spot. You've provided evidence she can't reasonably dispute, you've expressed concern for her and for the delegation, and you've asked that she come down off her defensive ramparts and talk. Waiting for an answer will itself turn up the challenge dial because silence is awkward.

Tempers may flare on both sides, in which case you should have a cooling-off period, but don't give up. Now that you've broached the subject directly you will work it out, especially if the two of you have a history of mutual commitment and honesty.

She's just overwhelmed

It may be that the two of you have been so caught up in the excitement of your project that Beth has neglected her other responsibilities and they have now caught up with her. You could increase support by sitting down and asking, "Okay, tell me all you've got to do at the moment and for whom?" After listening you could introduce a bit of challenge by saying, "So, from all this, what are the top priorities for you?" Sometimes that may be all that is needed to help her regroup and restart. But be careful. An invitation to the Cosy Club would be to rush in with, "Wow, you certainly have a lot on. Just prioritise these two items and leave the rest for another day." This increases your burden because those other things still have to get done, and Beth might be tempted to put them off indefinitely because you've tacitly admitted it's all too much. Soon you'll have to chase her, and be the bad guy, or do it yourself.

If you are Beth's only boss it may be in your power to wave your executive wand and take responsibilities from her and redistribute them among her colleagues, but you'll have to judge whether it is worth the kerfuffle of tampering with other people's workloads. A more interesting approach may be to have Beth herself start to delegate, in effect to begin doing what you're doing, with support from you, and learning along with you, so that radical accountability starts to spread.

It is impossible to give anything like a comprehensive answer to any of these scenarios because every person and situation is different, and feedback is an art, not a science. My objective here has been to give a flavour of the interplay between support and challenge and to show how both need to be ramped up in delegation.

Now, having established that feedback is truly meaningful only when there is genuine accountability, we'll return to the general topic of feedback with some selected tips because, in delegation, feedback must be skilful and plentiful both in the Feedback Conversation and around it.

Chapter 15 Reflections, ideas and tools

Reflection • What difficult conversation do you need to have but have been putting off because you don't want to upset the other person?

Idea • An ambitious delegation requires you to give lots of both support and challenge to the delegatee.

Idea • Too much challenge is the Zone of Stress, burn-out and uneven results. Too much support is the zone of complacency and slipping standards. Too little of each is the zone of inertia, apathy, isolation and boredom

Tool • Further reading: *Challenging Coaching*, by John Blakey and Ian Day (Nicholas Brealy Publishing, 2012)

CHAPTER 16
SEVEN MORE TIPS ON DELEGATION FEEDBACK

Most of what follows you already know. Lessons on how to behave and get along with others are learned from parents and at school, and swirl around our shared consciousness in the form of sayings and snippets of folk wisdom. Some have been penned by poets and pundits and have entered the language because they expressed a complex truth. To give some examples: "If you can't say anything nice, don't say anything at all" (meaning, what is the actual point of your criticism and blame, and what motivates it?); "Glass half full or half empty" (it's your choice whether you pick a positive interpretation or a negative one); "Don't kick a man when he's down" (rein in your cruelty); "Damn with faint praise" (the gap between false words and true feelings is visible to all); "Think positive" (attitudes affect outcomes, and attitudes can be adjusted).

In this sense we are all armchair experts on the subject of effective feedback. Like television sport commentators we can observe an interaction and spot what went wrong. ("Ah, look. See? That's what happens.") But when it is us in the fray do we follow the lessons we can recite from the armchair? Often, we don't. Often, we revert to habit and personal style, which are shaped by experience and the prevailing organisational culture.

The things we know about feedback are obvious before the encounter and after but can be distinctly *un*obvious in the heat of the moment.

Feedback is an art and mastering an art entails years of practice and reflection. We don't become expert archers by having archery accurately described to us. We have to do it and form new habits. So here are some tips on delegation feedback which you can practice. Consider them part of your field kit for fostering and nurturing radical accountability.

1. Feed back often, good and bad

Get into the habit of providing feedback regularly so you and the delegatee get used to it. It should be clear by now that annual appraisals are absurdly infrequent. Feedback for positive reasons as often as you do to point out failure. Feedback that comes only in response to a mishap loads it with negative baggage. "Offering input only when problems arise may cause people to see you as unappreciative or petty," observe the authors of *Giving Effective Feedback* (Harvard Business Review Press, Boston, Massachusetts, 2014). This is very astute. If people doubt your motives the cause is lost. Regularly praise not just successful outcomes but also to recognise effort, good ideas and innovative approaches. Find specific and genuine things to say, though, because general, overblown or ritualistic praise comes across as artificial and patronising. You might for instance identify the positive impact of what the delegatee has done, how it affects the project, and what others have said about it.

2. You are on the same team

Some people feel they must be combative when giving feedback, that feedback is essentially a clash of wills to be won or lost. It may be an approach learned in an aggressive milieu or a habit that has become ingrained out of a sense insecurity. Such an approach casts the delegatee as an adversary not as collaborator. The excuse is that 'trial by fire' is the best way to test the delegatee and to make him improve, as if the more horrible the experience, the harder he will work next time to avoid hurt and humiliation. It doesn't work: in modern organisations people will just leave if they are faced with unremitting hostility. The adversarial approach to management and feedback is largely outmoded now but traces can linger in us and creep back in under conditions of stress. It may be helpful periodically to run this check on your feedback style.

An adversarial approach:
- assumes the delegatee is shirking, lying, and concealing;
- probes for inconsistencies in what he says;
- tests him by using past failures as evidence of future failures;
- frames the encounter as an argument to be won or lost.

A collaborative approach:
- assumes the delegatee is doing his best with the tools and resources at hand;
- creates a comfortable space for him to disclose all and reflect on the emerging picture;
- nurtures confidence in him to promote excitement

and buy-in;
- frames the encounter as productive dialogue to uncover truth, ideas and useful insights.

3. Address the method, not the madness

Don't use feedback to try and improve someone, as in fix aspects of their character, no matter how irritated you may be by these perceived shortcomings. The authors of *Giving Effective Feedback* rank the following things from easiest to influence, to hardest to influence:

1. job skills (easiest)
2. time and work management
3. knowledge
4. attitudes
5. habits
6. personality traits (hardest)

Clearly, as you work down the list the closer you get to the other's sense of self, and self-esteem. That should be off-limits. It makes me think of the awful, fruitless, entrenched standoffs that have always occurred between parents and children, sparked by angry statements like "The problem with you is ..." Stick instead to areas that least threaten their sense of self-worth. That means tactics, knowledge, tricks, tips, work routines – their methods, in other words, not their 'madness'. This equips them to do a better job without attacking who they are.

4. Disrupt patterns of generalities

We've seen how the delegatee can retreat into generalities to ward you away from an area he feels uncomfortable with. This is normal human behaviour but if it develops into a pattern you will rightly begin to feel that you don't know what's really going on. Sometimes you can reinforce this pattern by using generalities yourself.

This was the experience of an executive I coached, let's call her Mary, who had successfully pitched the idea to her board for a substantial piece of customer relationship management software and was given responsibility for rolling it out. This she delegated to a talented marketing manager, who we'll call Will. After three months she grew tense and impatient because she was due to report to the board on the projected budget and schedule and Will seemed to be getting nowhere and furthermore was being persistently vague. When they next met, Will again ate up valuable time by going over in detail the pros and cons of various systems. Pressed on value for money, Will created more fog by describing how each solution was different, making a like-for-like comparison next to impossible. Pressed on cost, Will repeated that vendors had promised quotes which should come "any day now". No clearer, and feeling that Will was dithering, Mary steeled herself to get tough by repeating what she had said in the last two meetings, that "time is slipping away", and that Will was "bogging down" and must now "just get on with it" (generalities and clichés). But sensing that this would just make Will more defensive, causing him to retreat further into the mists of complexity, she switched tack and said: "Will, in four days I need to tell the board how this is going. I dread having to ask for more money and, with me not being able to give any indication of cost or time, they're going to think I'm leading us into one of those IT black holes. The whole thing will be cancelled, which means I'll look stupid and we won't get the software we need. I really want to show them we've got this in hand, so what can I tell them?"

A very different sort of conversation ensued. Presented with the particulars of her predicament (which was also his predicament), Will relented and admitted that he'd been hoping to come to her with the best deal all worked out, but that he'd become a bit lost and overwhelmed and had been playing for time. What followed was a purposeful chat in which it emerged that out of seven vendors there were three clear front-runners whose systems would be suitable, and early indications were that all three would be within range of the budget. Will agreed to give all three a forty-eight-hour deadline for firm quotes on the basis that they'd been shortlisted, and four days later Mary went to the board meeting with solid answers. The project was a success.

5. Offer suggestions instead of criticising

Instead of the feedback sandwich, which can be just a way of sweetening criticism, and tends to do more harm than good, try this deceptively simple technique for giving feedback which was developed by the Canadian Neuro-linguistic Programming trainer, Shelle Rose Charvet, and set out in her aptly titled essay, "The Feedback Sandwich Is Out To Lunch".[14] It goes like this:

---

14   Charvet, Shelle Rose, "The Feedback Sandwich Is Out To Lunch", (2008) *The OCM Coach-Mentor Journal.*

1. You make a suggestion.
2. You offer two reasons why it might work.
3. The first states what the suggested course of action would accomplish.
4. The second states what problem it would prevent.
5. You end with an encouraging comment.

Let's explore this in a scenario.

Robert is a young programmer who has been reporting to you for three months. One Monday you receive a call from your client, Jane, in which she complains about Robert. Jane says that her people are getting fed up with Robert because he doesn't listen. "He seems to make up his own ideas about what we want," Jane says. "They say they explain things to him – when they can get a word in edgewise – but there's always a twist in what he comes back with, something that isn't right. I sat in on a meeting on Friday and it was clear that he hadn't done what everybody thought was agreed. He's a nice guy and everybody likes him, and from a technical perspective he's excellent, but this isn't going to work unless he shuts up and starts to listen. Can I leave this with you?"

"Of course," you say, and hang up with a sinking feeling, because you recognise that in Robert, too. He is gifted, probably your best programmer, but is somewhat insecure and scatter-brained, and copes by talking a lot, which can present as boastful arrogance. So, you call a meeting with Robert. What are you going to say? You could do the tough-guy bit and hit him with blame and threats, but instead you decide to try Charvet's approach.

"Robert," you say when you're sitting down with him, "I've had a call from Jane saying her people are concerned because they feel there are gaps between what they've requested and what you're delivering. They say your work is good, but is sometimes not what they asked for. Can we talk about that for a minute? What are your thoughts on the working relationship?" This is a deeply uncomfortable way for Robert to start his week but his defensiveness eases when he sees that you're relaxed and ready to hear his side of the story. He starts by complaining that the client team knows nothing about programming, that they don't know what they want, and that they often give conflicting instructions. This is a common problem for contractors but, when you probe that by asking for examples, he doesn't offer any and switches instead to talking about how a programme like this needs to be done, something the client team "can't seem to understand". As you suspected, Robert is prone to getting wrapped up in his pursuit of technical beauty which, in his mind, can render the client team something of a nuisance. From the sheepish air that has now come over him you can see he knows this, really, and knows he's been caught out.

"If I may make a suggestion," you say, "in your meetings with Jane's people, try ending by summarising their require-ments as you've understood them, and also by summarising the actions that have been agreed (this is the helpful suggestion). From my experience, this reassures the client that you understand their requirements (reason one: what it will accomplish). It's also insurance for you against any claims that you haven't done what they've asked (reason two: the problem it will prevent). Meanwhile, don't worry. They like you. Plus, this is a normal concern for clients at this stage of a project, and you're a great fit for this one with your skills and experience (encouragement)."

This is better than the feedback sandwich because it isn't manipulative.

6. Listen actively

Feedback conversations in delegation will often be big, featuring heightened challenge and support. The conversations are not adversarial, but they will involve negotiation because you will each need help and commitment from the other. You will each want your views and concerns to be accepted as valid. Such conversations will often lead into the Zone of Uncomfortable Debate, described by Blakey and Day, and emotions will rise. If the two of you are not listening carefully, or 'actively' in the current jargon, misunderstandings can arise and opportunities for establishing common ground can be missed, leading to standoff, stalemate and soured feelings.

Active listening is sensibly proposed as a superior alternative to mere passive hearing. An internet search will bring up plenty of tips, but my favourites three are:

1. Prove you are listening by repeating back to the delegatee what he is saying, with, for instance, "So what you are saying is …", and "If I'm hearing you correctly …". This will calm emotions by assuring him that he is being heard and taken seriously. It also gives you time to think and to formulate questions that help him to clarify and examine his own position.

2. Defer hard and fixed judgement on his position until after

everything has been said and explored.

3. Don't fall for trigger words and phrases, which, intentionally or not, cause you offence or irritation. Keep focussing on what he is saying and its implications, not on the feelings welling up inside you; if you focus on your feelings you will miss things.

7. Everything is feedback

This is an aspect of delegation mindset. Everything is feedback. It could be the set of your shoulders, a glance at your phone, not acknowledging the delegatee in the corridor, a casual remark about the organisation or a customer, or a yawn: everything sends a signal about how you really feel and what you really think. To make sense of you, the delegatee will make up his own stories to interpret these signals and you may be unpleasantly surprised at the conclusions he draws. You may say that customers are important, but you send a different message if you disparage them. You may say you're interested in what the delegatee has to say but constantly checking your phone tells a different story. You're always communicating so it is best to take control and give the feedback you have chosen to give.

So far in this book we have talked mostly about you and the delegatee as if you can operate in laboratory conditions. As a swimmer, I would use the metaphor of a swimming relay event comprising just the two of you in a pool. You do ten lengths, then he does ten lengths, and on you go until the end. There is only one of you in the pool at a time, so the water is smooth and the direction is clear: you just follow the fat black line on the bottom.

The real world is not like that. It is more like the start of the swim section of my first-ever Ironman triathlon. Picture 1,200 edgy, hyped-up competitors all piling into the water at once, all going for the same line – the shortest distance to the finish – as fast as they possibly can. It was mayhem! I was kicked and punched, my goggles were knocked down over my nose, and I swallowed several mouthfuls of the freezing North Sea. There was no black line to follow, only blackness below and, inches in front of my face, the thrashing feet of swimmers who may or may not have been going in the right direction. Delegation in organisational life is more like this – chaotic and turbulent – than the orderly relay in the swimming pool. It is so because of systems and the next and final section is about navigating your way through them.

Chapter 16 Reflections, ideas and tools

Tools • Seven more tips on delegation feedback:

1. *Feed back often, good and bad*: Get into the habit of providing feedback regularly, so you both get used to it.
2. *You are on the same team*: Check your feedback style and assumptions. Are you being adversarial or collaborative?
3. *Address the method, not the madness*: Don't use feedback to try and fix aspects of his character. That attacks a person's sense of self-worth. Stick to tactics, knowledge, tips, and work routines.
4. *Disrupt patterns of generalities*: Vague and evasive language can undermine feedback; learn to spot and challenge it.
5. *Offer suggestions instead of criticising*: Instead of using the feedback sandwich to sweeten criticism, make a suggestion and offer two reasons why it might work.
6. *Everything is feedback*: You're always communicating, so take control and give the feedback you have chosen to give.

PART FIVE:
SYSTEMS AND ALL THAT GETS IN THE WAY

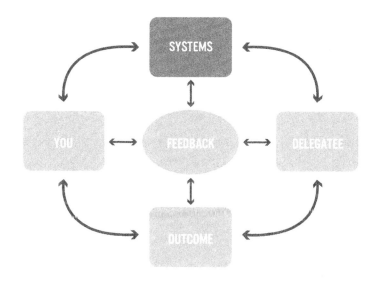

Overview

Delegation never happens in a vacuum. Through systems, the world will always interfere and can sometimes seem to do its best to scupper our endeavours. Systems are defined here as forces – personal, social, physical, economic, political, and more – that exert influence on us. The influence we have over them is weak and gets weaker the farther out from our own little worlds we look. However, even systems we cannot control do reach in to meddle with us. We will use the case study of a rising young star called Jason, who was dragged down by systems, to explore how the delegator and the delegatee can mount a response to them. First you both need to adjust your mindset to be aware of them, and a way of interrogating the impact of systems in our concentric zones of influence is proposed here.

A systems perspective is liberating because it allows you to avoid the trap of blaming failure on individuals, or on other single events or elements. As we'll explore, it is not the things themselves that are most important but rather the relationships between things.

Because system forces ripple along to us through the medium of people, the best way to rebel against the tyranny of systems is through relationships: we need the right relationships with the right people, and one way you can support the delegatee is by providing relationship air cover.

I argue further in this section that results flow most reliably not from hard and fast action but from relationships. The most important relationship in the delegation is between you and the delegatee and, in order to achieve big results, that relationship and other core relationships in the delegation need to be big if they are to resist the negative influence of systems. A definition of bigness in that sense is proposed.

CHAPTER 17
HOW THE WORLD WILL MESS WITH YOU

Let's imagine for a moment that you've been implementing the ideas in this book as you read. You should now be at an exciting juncture. You've identified what you're going to delegate; you've carefully framed it in SMART or Courageous terms; you've selected your delegatee and, thanks to the Trustworthy Tracker, you have confidence in his ability to do the job. He may even have got started and the two of you have had some Delegation Feedback Conversations, and they were productive. He is off, all is in hand, and you can rest easy … right? Wrong, of course. It's not that simple. Your delegation project is going to encounter the world, and the world, as it always does, will mess with you.

To help us tackle this challenge, I propose that we think of the world in terms of systems. By systems I mean the interlinked networks of forces that influence everything we do: political systems, people systems, economic systems, environmental systems, technological systems, even internal, psychological systems. For instance, I may work in a team, which is a system. My team is part of a department, which is also a system. My department is one of several in a company. My company is in a particular industry or sector. That sector operates in an environment influenced by geographical, economic and political systems.

This is a crude map and in making it we have already missed other intersecting systems that exert influence at every level: from culture, technology and hard systems (physical surroundings and infrastructure) to acts of God. To complicate things further I, myself, am a system of physical and psychological systems.

The degree of influence we have over these systems varies, from sometimes rather a lot (me), to quite a bit (my team), to some (my department), before falling off rapidly to pretty much none at all (think of the oil price, geopolitics, and financial markets). And in this sense systems are unfair because systems which we do not understand and over which we have no control can have drastic impacts on us, such as when a strike by air traffic controllers ruins my holiday or when panic in financial markets leads to the collapse of my customer base.

This makes life complex. To appreciate how complex, we could ponder the notion of Combinatorial Explosion, where a set of variables combine with another set of variables and the numbers involved expand exponentially, and very fast. For instance, you are about to get dressed and have ten items of clothing. Free of norms and conventions, you can put shoes on your hands and your shirt on top of your coat. How many different sartorial combinations are available? Twenty or thirty? No, there are over three and a half million (the maths is factorial ten). Add in another item of clothing and you have just under forty million. Make it twelve, and your options rise to just over 479 million (factorial 11 and 12 respectively).

Fortunately, Combinatorial Explosion need not apply to people working together. If it did, the outcome of a day in the life of a team of twelve people would be utterly random, and it isn't, normally: people do come together and bend to a common purpose. But keep in mind that we are each, as individuals, complex systems. I have been trying to comprehend myself for over half a century, with only patchy success; truly comprehending other people is probably impossible. And if you have twelve people in your local system and each of them is a complex system interacting with complex systems beyond your view, expressing or predicting how exactly your local system will behave on contact with other local systems is tricky. I would further argue that in our splintered organisational world, systems have proliferated (that is, there are more of them), and they have become harder to map. I suspect that our frustration over how hard it can be to 'get things done around here' stems from a lack of appreciation of systems. For deep and deliberate delegation to work, delegator and delegatee must be aware of systems and get feedback from them in order to mount a response.

How does this play out in real life? The following is a case study drawn from my practice. It is true, in the sense that the dynamics accurately depict real life, but the events and characters are assembled from a variety of case studies, and the names and companies are not real in order to maintain confidentiality.

Meet Jason, a thirty-two-year-old engineer, bright, keen, married with two young children, recently promoted to the role of project manager at the company he has worked for since leaving college, a contractor called MT (Northern) Ltd. I got to know Jason and his story while helping the managing director of MT develop a strategic plan for his board. With his promotion, Jason has been put in sole charge of his first project, a groundworks civil engineering contract for phase one of a multi-million-pound expansion of the harbour at Aberdeen, Scotland. It is not a major project for the company in terms of size, but it is important because it could lead to more work in subsequent phases. In the bigger picture, port infrastructure work is expanding in Scotland and MT, struggling with some unprofitable projects won in the recession, needs to get a piece of that pie.

Jason is excited by his new responsibility although he is a little anxious because he reports to Steve, a brusque operations director parachuted in two years ago from London to drive business expansion in the north. Steve, our delegator, is what we might call 'old school', relishing the traditionally aggressive approach to the contracting business.

Despite his excitement Jason is soon overwhelmed. He must mobilise the project quickly, which means organising site cabins and kitting them out with power, telecoms and furniture. Because the job is relatively small he is not given any admin support and because MT has just won several other projects there is no space for him at head office and he must share an office at another project fifteen miles out of Aberdeen. This is an extra headache for Jason who lives sixty miles to the south in Dundee, where MT's regional HQ is.

It is not ideal but Jason cracks on. Among his top priorities is producing a detailed plan – a programme – for the work and, following procedure, he goes to Paul, who is MT's planning manager and asks Paul to produce one. "Leave it with me," Paul says and off Jason goes to tackle everything else on his to-do list. He expects his programme to arrive in a matter of days. Paul, meanwhile, has a team of six specialist planners who programme all the company's work. This team is also flat out because of the sudden avalanche of projects. Paul delegates Jason's programme to Anthony who has been brought in from an agency to help. In his way, Anthony is also old school. He likes to lay out full-scale printed drawings so he can see the whole picture but there isn't room for that in the company's hot-desking office set up, so he has to struggle over a laptop, which slows him down.

Two weeks later, Jason calls Paul to find out where his programme is. Paul explains that his department is snowed under but says he'll get Anthony, the agency guy, to call in a day or so with an update. Paul forgets to tell Anthony. In the meantime, Paul meets with Steve, the brusque operations director, who tells him among a dozen other things that Jason should do his own programme as it's not a big project and Jason is pretty good at doing programmes. Neither tells Jason. Two more weeks pass and there is still no programme. Jason has left messages with Anthony but with gear now arriving on his site he has plenty else to think about.

Contractually, Jason had to submit the programme to the client within four weeks and midway through week five the client rings Steve to find out where it is. "Leave it with me," Steve growls, "I'll get back to you by close of play tomorrow." Steve immediately calls Jason demanding to know what's going on. Jason, taken aback, says has been waiting on the planning department for a month and can't get through to this Anthony person. "No, no, no," says Steve, his voice rising, "we agreed you'd do the programme yourself. You need to get it in by the end of this week or we've got an issue." Jason is stunned by Steve's response but before he can collect his wits in comes another curve ball. Jane, his wife, a freelance events manager, calls to say that their youngest is ill and needs picking up from school and she is on her way to a meeting with a major new client in Edinburgh. Jason must drop everything and head back down to Dundee.

With his little boy finally tucked into bed (he has the flu) Jason starts to seethe. He is barely coping with setting up the harbour wall job on his own and now out of the blue he must do his own programme by the end of the week, which is practically impossible. Worse, Steve has blamed him for causing trouble. He is sitting at the kitchen table trying to catch up on some urgent email correspondence when he gets another call, this time from a head-hunter. It is the second call from this particular recruiter, who is very determined to poach him for another company. Other head-hunters have called as well. With infrastructure work on the rise across the country and with talent so scarce in the industry people like Jason are hot property. So far, he has ignored these approaches. He always felt loyal to MT, which sponsored his degree and for a period gave him mentoring as a pathway to management. Now it feels like a different company and he finds he is listening to the smooth voice on the phone. There would be a flash new car and work guaranteed close to home. "And I shouldn't say this," the recruiter says, "but, between you and me, I think you could basically name your price."

Three days later, it is not the programme Jason hands over to Steve but his resignation.

Chapter 17 Reflections, ideas and tools

Reflection • What caused Jason to resign? Poor communication? Bad management? Company over-reach? A lack of support? His own lack of experience? When no single factor seems to be an adequate explanation it is time to start paying attention to systems.

Idea • Delegation never happens in a vacuum; through systems the world will interfere. Systems are interlinked networks of forces that impinge on our puny zones of influence. They can be political, economic, social, environmental, technological or even internal and psychological. They include our physical surroundings and the culture and behaviours of our customers.

Idea • The influence we exert over systems weakens quickly the farther out we go from our zones of influence. It doesn't work the other way around, though, because systems over which we have no control can have a major impact on us, and on our delegation.

Idea • If we're not aware of systems, they can ambush us.

CHAPTER 18
WHAT JUST HAPPENED? MAPPING SYSTEMS

In days gone by at MT the sudden departure of a junior project manager would have been just one of those things. Not any longer: this was a calamity. The Aberdeen project was an important foothold in an expanding market and a route out of trouble for the company. Like other contractors, MT was losing money on risky commercial projects it had won by bidding low during the recession. As always, when you buy work in this way some of these projects had turned toxic, with MT having to take the hit for higher-than-budgeted costs, leading to delays and disputes with the client. Such projects can bring companies down and MT was not immune. It saw port infrastructure as a stable sector that could help offset the losses that the toxic projects would inflict for the next several years. Aberdeen was the proving ground and it wasn't much of an exaggeration to say that Jason was the only person who could do it. Across the industry, talent was getting scarcer and MT, as we've seen, was already over-extended.

Steve reacted badly to Jason's resignation. He was angry and his passive aggressive response suggested that Jason lacked loyalty and had been promoted beyond his abilities. Jason blew up, saying Steve was the reason he was leaving and accusing Steve of steering the company to ruin, before storming out. When word of Jason's departure reached Rob, the managing director of MT and my contact, Rob was alarmed, then furious. To have the project manager resign one month into the contract made MT look terrible. Who would replace Jason? Everybody was fully deployed already and pulling someone in off the street would be costly and risky. It would mean delays as the new person got up to speed, and delays meant disputes – all this while MT was trying to make a good impression. He ordered Steve to call Jason right away and apologise and to ask Jason not to tell the client he was leaving until MT worked out the best way forward. Suitably chastened, Steve complied.

This is when Rob contacted me. He'd hatched a plan to conduct a detailed exit interview with Jason to discover what had led to his decision to resign and what the company could learn from it. He said it was relevant to the work I was doing with the board because, if the company could not hang on to its talent, something was very wrong. "What's the point of developing a strategy, Dave," he said bitterly, "if there's not going to be anybody left to implement it?" Rob felt that Jason might be more comfortable talking to me as a third party. He also confessed to having an ulterior motive: if we could understand why Jason left, we stood a better chance of putting things right and convincing him to stay. I agreed.

From preliminary conversations with Steve, Paul and Jason it was clear that, as a delegation, Jason's project was compromised from the start. There was no effective feedback between Steve (the delegator) and Jason (the delegatee) and the conditions necessary for good accountability on Jason's part had quickly eroded, in the sense that the tools Jason assumed he would have in the form of help from MT's planning department were withdrawn. Nevertheless, given his reputation for dedication and hard work, Jason's decision to resign just five weeks into his dream assignment seemed disproportionate. So, guided by the old adage that an argument is never about what it is about, I decided to conduct Jason's exit interview as a systems analysis.

We have probably all come across instances of dysfunction such as that which affected Jason and the temptation is usually to pin blame on particular elements of the dysfunction, such as the breakdown of communication between Jason, Paul and Steve, or on particular people. Impatient for answers, we might conclude that Jason is out of his depth, or that Paul is negligent, or that Anthony just can't keep up, or that Steve is a bully. But this is simplistic. It may even be simplistic to blame the combination of these particular factors. In her book, *Executive Coaching with Backbone and Heart*, Mary Beth O'Neill proposes that a systems perspective 'resists identifying a single element or person in a system as being the root cause of the problem'. A system is made up of interdependent, interacting parts, where changes in one part create changes in other parts. Deep and deliberate delegation requires getting feedback from systems. We must understand them because they have the power to scupper our endeavour, but that requires you and the delegatee to be aware of them in the first place. With that in mind, and given that my responsibility was to Rob and the board, I judged that the one who most needed to hear this was Steve, so I suggested that he sit in, if Jason agreed. To their credit, both did.

My plan was to apply an approach to systems mapping taught

to me by one of my own coaches, Alison Whybrow.[15] It is very relevant to delegation. It identifies seven lenses through which participants can observe and interrogate the systems that impinge on their performance. The lenses correspond to seven zones of immediacy, starting with your own physical work environment and radiating outward into the world. This isn't a philosophical assertion concerning the nature of phenomena, but simply a tool you can use to start thinking about all the stuff that gets in the way, much of it intangible or not immediately obvious. When Jason, Steve and I sat down together the following week, I explained this, and what I wanted to do. They looked a bit baffled, so I suggested we just get started.

THE SEVEN SYSTEM LENSES

Lens 1: Your physical work environment

When I asked Jason to describe his office, and what it was like, he was even more baffled. "I know it might seem trivial," I said, "and it may turn out to be, but we need to be thorough, and our work environment has a big influence on how we feel and perform. So, if you can, try and describe it."

Jason thought for a moment, then sat up. "Well actually, Dave, it was a nightmare," he said. "I was told there wasn't any room at head office, and so I had to share a site cabin with John Graham, who's building a school in Newburgh. I'm on the phone, trying

---

15   The approach was developed by Peter Hawkins and Nick Smith in their book, *Coaching, Mentoring and Organizational Consultancy: Supervision, Skills & Development*, 2nd Ed. (Open University Press, 2013)

to get mobilised, organising cabins, phones, furniture, all the equipment, and it's clearly getting on John's nerves. He's already short on space. We were actually sharing a desk. I felt for John but what could I do? Sometimes I'd go to the car to make calls, but I needed my laptop, too. It was a joke. I spoke to Steve about it, but he said, basically, 'tough, get over it', which I can understand, I guess. We're sort of running everything on a shoestring at the moment. But it's not right. I felt like I was in everybody's way. Plus, Newburgh's another half hour's drive north of Aberdeen, so I'm spending four hours driving back and forth every day."

Steve shifted uncomfortably but kept quiet, as I'd requested. He wasn't meant to have a major speaking part in this exercise.

Lens 2: Your work culture

Next, I asked Jason to describe the culture of MT, as it seemed to him. How did people speak and behave toward each other? What are the relationships like? What are the values and assumptions?

"Well," he said, warming up, "looking back, it used to be good. I've been here since I graduated and there was a calm, organised feel to the set up. We were the good guys. Maybe because it's a smaller world up here compared to London or Manchester, but we made sure we got along with the clients and the subcontractors. If there was ever an issue we'd be on the phone or setting up a meeting right away to get it sorted before it started to fester. It was a business built on trust. Then there was the recession and we got a new MD and new guys coming in – sorry Steve – and now there's a real edge. Huge pressure to win jobs, which means bidding low and then cutting corners and playing dirty to claw back money from them. I can see people, subcontractors, looking at us, going, 'oh, it's like that now, is it?' It's not what I'm used to. It's horrible."

This was going well. Jason had a lot to get off his chest. I tried not to look at Steve.

Lens 3: The people who matter

Still at the company level, I asked Jason to talk about the people around him, those who had a stake in his success and the success of the organisation, both up and down the chain of seniority. What do they think? How did they engage? What did success look like for them?

"First off, I don't have anyone reporting in to me," Jason said. "Steve said this is a small project and that I should be able to do it 'one man and his dog style' – in other words on my own. I have to say, this is totally counterproductive. I am doing loads that could be done by a technician or a recent graduate. So, I'm swamped. Getting site cabins in isn't rocket science. I'd like to have time to think strategically about the project, so the client feels confident, and, you know, impressed, but I can't get to that because I'm stuck on the end of John's desk making calls and bugging him. Then I get dumped with the programme. As for Steve, I'm not sure what he thinks. That I'm not very good, I guess. Maybe it's possible to do a good job under these circumstances. Maybe someone could have shown me how."

Steve at that point was looking out the window with an expression I couldn't read.

"And what about your family, Jason," I said. "They matter too, obviously."

Jason hesitated, and then said: "It's hard, to be honest. Jane, my wife, is trying to get her business off the ground. Things are starting to pick up for her. She stayed home for the kids but the youngest is in school this year, so she's going for it, and I always promised to support her plans. My mum and dad are nearby to help out but they're getting on and we don't take them for granted. So, it's all a bit up in the air just now, especially with me working all hours to get Aberdeen off the ground. It's really stressful. Money's an issue, too. The landlord is whacking the rent up. We're trying save to buy something, but it isn't happening, and probably won't until Jane's thing takes off. We went on a little package holiday two years ago, and that's it. I worry the kids are missing out."

"So," Jason said, after a pause, and glancing over at Steve, "I guess you can see why I'm attracted to this other job."

Lens 4: Your organisation and its customers

I moved the focus outward, to the systems MT operated in. What, I asked, are the ambient concerns and challenges? What are MT's customers like? What are their values and behaviour? What are MT's suppliers like?

"That's more a question for Steve, isn't it?" Jason said.

"Not entirely," I said. "Remember, we need to get feedback from the systems that influence us. On the Aberdeen project, you're six weeks into an engagement with a client who is new to MT, in a sector that is also new, so you're intersecting with new systems and on that subject in this room right now you're the expert."

"Right, okay," said Jason. "Well, on this job our client is actually a massive German outfit, Bauen, which is the main contractor, so we're subcontracted to them, which is a bit unusual for us. They have a procedure for absolutely everything. It's very regimented. At first, I thought it was crazy, the forms I had to fill out on site access protocols and health and safety and method-ologies for this and that. It's one of the reasons I'm so behind. They also do everything electronically, which took some getting used to. But actually, I can see the point of it. They're drilling down to a level of detail at the outset we normally don't think about until later. It's tedious, but then you realise that a lot of the issues that can come back to bite you in the bum are getting taken care of. They're way ahead of us and it made me feel like a bit of a bumpkin."

"Interesting," I said. "Anything else?" I could see that Steve was listening intently.

"Yes, actually, the overall client is the port. It's what they call a trust port, which means it's not a private company and any profits go back into the port's development, which is meant to be for the public benefit. They take it very seriously. This is a huge expansion and they want the project itself to be positive and professional. They're under the gun for time, too, because there is a lot of North Sea oil platform decommissioning coming on stream, so they need to be ready for that. A safety incident or a stupid delay would reflect badly on everyone. It all left me feeling that we needed to up our game, which was stressful because I was just flat out trying to cope with what was in front of me."

Lens 5: The sector view

"Thanks for that, Jason," I said. Steve was busy making notes. "Now, let's broaden it out to the sector you're operating in, infrastructure. What are the trends and pressures there?"

"This is a really weird time," Jason said. "You've got huge projects all over the country and everyone's racing for a piece of the action, which means bidding low to win the work, which is what we did at Aberdeen. It's an open secret. My guy at Bauen, Frank, actually admitted that he'd wanted the second-place bidder to win the job because he'd worked with them before and trusted them whereas we're the new kids on the block. The view is, we're too cheap and untested. He's a nice guy but he made it clear that at the first slip up he'll try to get us out and the other guys in.

"The other side of it is that everybody's overstretched because the workforce is shrinking. People are getting older and young blood isn't coming in. I read somewhere that over half the industry is over fifty, which means a big chunk of people are retiring every year and they are not getting replaced. Which I guess explains why I've got recruiters on the phone every two minutes. When you're overstretched, things go wrong. Mistakes, accidents, the lot, and that means big financial risks. Health and safety now is really scary because there are new sentencing guidelines and companies are getting fined millions when accidents happen, whereas it was a rap on the knuckles before.

"Generally, everybody's obsessed with watching their backs. Things have got uber-contractual. It used to be the actual contract went in the drawer and you all just got on with the job. Now we're bombarded with petty emails from clients and subcontractors with huge attachments so that if anything goes wrong in six months they can say, well, didn't you read the document I sent you? You can spend all day trying to read the small print and it's all just legal gobbledygook. I keep thinking, come on, Jason, get organised. As project manager, it's down to me. It feels like a sword's hanging over my head."

Lens 6: The national view

"That's useful, thanks," I said, feeling glad that I was not in his shoes. "Okay, we're nearly there. Now I'd like you to take a national view, if you can. What are some of the bigger issues – political, economic, social, technical, environmental – that are shaping the background now?"

"Phew, well, everything's up in the air, for a start," Jason said. "Obviously, there's Brexit, and nobody really knows yet what impact that's going to have, and the possibility of Scottish independence means a double whammy of uncertainty. There are rumours that big commercial property and retail schemes are being put on hold while investors wait to see which way the wind is going to blow. Infrastructure seems to be a safer bet, which means MT will really have to make a reputation for itself there in the next few years."

Lens 7: The global view

It was time for the final lens. I asked Jason what dynamics at a global level were having an impact on MT locally.

"Wow, Dave," he said. "That's a bit 'out there', isn't it?"

I laughed. "Hey, you're lucky we're not going into space. Some people believe solar cycles and sunspots affect financial markets, but we'll stick to Earth for now. I'm just asking you to think about it, Jason. Systems affect us, local systems and global systems, and the more we're aware of this, the better we can respond."

"Well," said Jason, "come to think of it, Frank at Bauen has been after me about precautions against terrorism. Apparently, it's in the contract and we have to submit a strategy for it along with our programme. I asked Steve about it, but he just said don't worry, it's not down to us. But Frank showed me the clause and it is down to us. That's way out of my league. How am I supposed to put a strategy together for that? I really didn't sign up for this."

Steve had stopped writing. He had his elbows on the table and was holding his head, as if lost in thought, or in despair.

"Ok Jason, that's great," I said. "You've given us lots to think about. It's all extremely relevant and helpful, so thank you. Now, that brings to a close my formal role in this interview, so we're done, unless Steve has something to add at this point. Steve?"

Steve roused himself, ran his hands down his face, and sighed.

"Yes, well, Jason," he said. "I actually don't know what to say." He was quiet for what seemed like an age, tapping his pen on his pad. "I mean, I knew about the port and what it all meant, vaguely, but, wow, you've just made it real."

Steve tapped some more, and then seemed to make up his mind.

"When you began, my hackles went up. I wanted to say, hang on, you have no idea what it's like from where I'm sitting, the pressure I'm under, the pressure the company's under, with shareholders breathing down our necks and what not. But that's no excuse. You were under huge pressure, too, and I'm ashamed to think how we didn't support you. When I was your age it was a different culture. When we were in a tight spot we just did everything harder and faster and hoped it would all come right in the end. Families were for Christmas and Easter."

At this he looked down and shook his head, giving a rueful laugh.

"I want to apologise to you, Jason," looking at the younger man for the first time. "And I want to tell you that you are the person to do this job. Not only that: when I listen to you speak, I realise that you are the person to use this job to help us change, to up MT's game, as you put it. It is clear to me now what this project, with you leading it, means for the company, and what's at stake. It would be a tragedy if you left. Rob knows we're talking here today and he has authorised me to try and convince you to stay. I wasn't sure how to do that. All I could think was, 'how much more money does he want?' Pathetic, isn't it? Now I have some ideas. We will elevate the status of this project and rally behind you on it. We will find you an assistant and pay you to train them as your deputy, so that in due course you don't have to be on site or in the office every minute of the day. You can work from home when it suits you. We'll line up legal, contractual and planning advice and support so that you're not bogged down by those issues and so you can be in front of the client as much as you need to be, and be properly prepared. We'll ask you to advise us on the process innovations you're witnessing. You will have a direct line to the board. We'll review your salary so that it reflects your importance to this project, and to the future of the company."

Steve stopped then, and sat back. He was clearly emotional. I hadn't warmed to Steve but just now he had spoken from the heart. We were of the same generation, coming of age in the industry when it was taken as read that you worked yourself to death for the company. I knew, too, that he was going through a divorce.

"I don't know, Steve. It's all a bit late for that," said Jason. He looked angry and upset. "This feels like crocodile tears. You guys are in a bind, but it's not my problem anymore. The number of times I brought all this up with you ... why should I believe anything would change?" He stood up to go. "I don't want to talk about it, to be honest. Maybe I'll think about it."
And he left.

Chapter 18 Reflections, ideas and tools

Reflection • Have you ever asked yourself, "Why is it so hard to get anything done around here?" A systems perspective avoids the trap of always attributing failure to particular individuals, or other single events or elements.

Idea • Getting feedback from systems helps you respond to their influence and protect the outcome of your delegation.

Tool • Understand systems better by interrogating their influence through the Seven System Lenses. They are: 1) Your physical work environment; 2) Your work culture; 3) The relationships that matter; 4) Your organisation and its customers; 5) Your sector; 6) The national view; 7) The global view.

Tool • Map your systems: It can be helpful to visualise things. This is a way for you and the delegatee to map the systems that are influencing your delegation, so you can both gain a better understanding of what is going on. Start with a blank piece of paper and draw simple objects to represent people, things, issues or events that have an impact on the delegation. Expand and explore rather than try to get it 'right'. Use arrows to indicate the direction in which people seem most to be facing, and use space between the objects to represent proximity and strength of relationship: close is close and distant is distant. The result is likely to be messy and will probably be meaningless to an outsider, but it will spark discussion and discovery for you and the delegatee. Initially, the objective is to represent 'what is' rather than 'what should be'.

Here is Jason's map before his resignation. There was a lot going on: Frank, the client's representative, was 'in his face' demanding action while his colleagues Steve, Rob, Paul, and Anthony were distant and facing the company (MT), not him and his project. That meant they were not facing an important customer of MT. Jason felt deserted. Even Jane, his wife, was facing away, trying to get her business off the ground. His parents and children were looking to him for help, although he was struggling to cope. The only person who seemed to be looking out for his interests was the head-hunter, which meant Jason was distracted from the project, looking toward better prospects elsewhere. In Jason's mind there was only one thing to do: jump ship. After our meeting, I asked Jason what would be better and in a few moves, he turned Steve, Rob, Paul and MT around and pulled them all closer, so they were focussed, as he was, on Frank, the customer. He deleted the head-hunter. "There, that feels better," he said. "I'm staying."

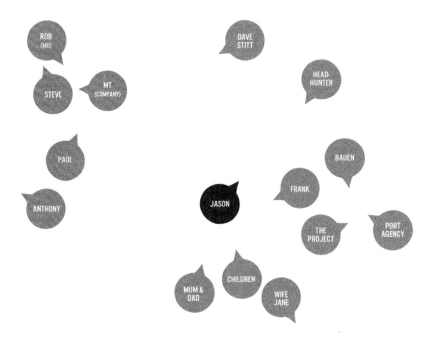

FIGURE 5. Jason's systems map (Credit: Dave Stitt)

Tool • For more information, see *Systemic Coaching & Constellations*, by John Whittington (2nd ed., 2016).

CHAPTER 19
REBEL AGAINST SYSTEMS THROUGH RELATIONSHIPS

Steve thought of himself as a results-oriented guy, a man of action, a no-nonsense operator. I knew the type, because I used to think of myself in the same way. Our mindset would have been summed up by: "When the going gets tough, the tough get going." Put another way, hard-to-achieve results required hard work and actions that not everyone was typically prepared to take. He and I would work crazy hours and make others do the same. We would pile all kinds of pressure on people we felt were not pulling their weight. Sometimes, to manage clients and sub-contractors, it seemed necessary to bend the truth or manipulate people and situations. Other times we would gamble on risky shortcuts. Big results required bold actions: work harder and faster, we would say. We got results – meaning the thing (usually) got built and we (usually) stayed out of court and avoided bank-ruptcy – but there were always costs. These costs included soured customer relationships, high staff turnover, bad blood between us and suppliers, our own high stress levels, burn-out, and damaging strain on our family lives. In the industry culture of the time, however, such costs were considered the norm.

In the 1990s, the UK construction industry came under

intense pressure to reform because, as a sector, its performance was appalling, with cost overruns, waste and delays
more the rule than the exception. This became a political issue
because one of the biggest users of the construction industry
is government, which, at the national and local levels, relies on
the construction industry to deliver schools, hospitals, roads,
railways and other public assets. And government, quite rightly,
was fed up with the service it was receiving. A main problem
identified with the industry was its adversarial and aggressive
culture. So, in that context, I was selected to help lead a culture
change programme at the company I worked for, a national
contractor. Experts were brought in from outside, and my eyes
were opened to entirely new ways of thinking. I was fascinated
by this. In the process, I was introduced to a concept developed
by the American thinker, Werner Erhard, that analysed the
origins of organisational results, and which proposed relationships as their ultimate source and foundation. This simple
concept, which I'll call the Results Pyramid, hit me like a bolt
of lightning. So obvious and yet so foreign to my habitual
way of thinking, it changed my life and became the bedrock
of my approach to team and organisational development. I'd
like to spend a little time exploring the model now because it
can guide us in navigating our delegation project through the
swirling currents of systems.[16]

---

16   Some of the materials in this chapter, specifically the Results Pyramid, are
the property of Landmark Worlwide LLC and Werner Erhard, and are used with
permission.

FIGURE 6. The Results Pyramid: Everything flows from relationships (Credit: Werner Erhard)

In order to achieve results, we must take actions. This much is clear to men of action like Steve and me, but our understanding was shallow. The thinking behind the Results Pyramid suggests that results flow most reliably out of relationships, which produce possibilities, which in turn activate opportunities, which enable action. This is somewhat abstract, so here is a little scenario that might help illustrate the concept.

Let us say that near my house there is a dangerous junction. In the past year there have been four accidents at this junction, with the most recent occurring last night: I'd heard the dreadful bang from my living room. Thankfully, no one was hurt, but I know that it is only a matter of time before someone does get hurt, or worse. Today, I can't stop thinking about it, and, being a man of action, I resolve to go into town and speak to the mayor, who holds public consultations on Wednesdays. I'm going to make him put up a stop sign. Into my car I get, and off I go.

To me, this seems a reasonable course of action. I've discerned a possibility – a stop sign – and I have a relationship with the mayor, in the sense that he is my mayor, and I am his citizen. But the meeting goes badly. The mayor is patronising, dismissive, and refuses to consider a stop sign. "It's not in the budget," he says. I drive home, fuming, and I continue to fume for the rest of the day. Then I resolve to take more action. I write a poster – 'No More Accidents: Stop Sign Here, Now!' – and march out to the junction, waving it at passing cars and shouting my slogan. But all I get are looks of hostility or indifference from the people in the cars rushing past. It starts to rain. After a couple of hours, I trudge home, tired, wet and dispirited.

"What is the matter with these people?" I say to my wife that night. "Don't they realise someone is going to get killed?"

"Why don't you organise a local meeting or something," she says before falling asleep.

Oh, great, a local meeting, I think. What's the point of that?

But, lacking any other plan, I do organise a meeting. I write a letter outlining my concerns and inviting people to the village hall next week to discuss the issue. I make copies and hand-deliver them to the fifty or so houses in the neighbourhood. On the night, only a handful show up, and they are not the sparkiest bunch I've ever seen. Mabel, in her eighties, wants to talk about litter. Nigel, also elderly, seems determined to reminisce at length about the area before all the houses were built. Victoria, the youngest, sits hunched into her coat, saying nothing, while the other two, June and Melissa, seem to have come only for the gossip and biscuits. After half an hour of aimless chit-chat, I'm ready to go home.

Then Mabel claps her hands.

"Right folks," she says, "young Dave here is raring to go on this stop sign business, so let's put our heads together. I was thinking we could set up a Facebook page. My daughter's always campaigning for this and that on Facebook. She's very keen."

Then Nigel says he used to work for the council as a planner, and knows where to find all the data on road accidents. If it showed our junction to be a trouble spot, that would make interesting reading on the Facebook page. June pipes up, saying she could start raising money through an online crowd-funding site to pay for leaflets. Melissa knows people at the local TV station, and could maybe organise some coverage.

Mabel, meanwhile, has been talking quietly to Victoria. "Go on, tell them, Victoria," Mabel says.

"I can make videos," Victoria says, speaking for the first time. "We could do a video explaining why we need a stop sign."

"We could put it on the Facebook page," says Mabel. "It might go viral!"

For another hour, ideas fly back and forth, and plans are hatched, and I go home exhilarated, with all the ingredients of a campaign in place.

Let's look again at the Results Pyramid. Possibilities arise out of relationships among people. The 'web of human relationships', to use a term explored by the political philosopher, Hannah Arendt (1906–1975), literally covers the world. In its entirety, it seems infinite and unmappable to us individuals, but we are still each a part of it, and out of this web arises all that is possible in human affairs, from world peace to Armageddon and everything in between – including our stop sign.

My first action, going to see the mayor, bore no fruit because my relationship with him was weak. I am only one of many citizens, and he owes no special obligation to me. But when I activated my local web of human relationships, interesting and unforeseen possibilities began to emerge. These possibilities can then be actualised by the opportunities available: the hardware, software, data, skills, contacts, time and effort at our group's disposal. The action that follows – the launch our campaign – could create pressure on the mayor that he cannot ignore and then – result! – a stop sign.

The lesson contained in this little scenario will be familiar to everyone: big things happen when people come together. A broader relationship base leads to more potent possibilities, which in turn leads to more diverse opportunities and more effective actions. In theory, this is so obvious it is a cliché, but in reality, it is widely ignored in organisational life; at work we often behave as if it doesn't apply. Men of action like Steve and (formerly) me tend to think exclusively in terms of action, without giving any thought to relationships, or, worse, to the damage our actions can do to relationships. (When I was a young project manager I once found *Dave Stitt is a bastard!* scrawled on the wall of the portable toilet; I hate to say it now, but it made me feel proud.) Meanwhile, we wonder why everything is so stressful and hard.

This emphasis on results to the exclusion of relationships turns the Results Pyramid on its head, and the consequence is stress and instability, as Paul Fox, a fellow coach, articulated powerfully in this diagram.

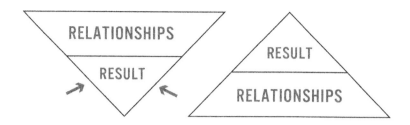

FIGURE 7. Turning the Results Pyramid upside down leads to instability (Credit: Paul Fox)

In the left pyramid all the effort goes into the Result. People are busy getting on with their function, and little time is spent on developing relationships. The whole structure is unstable, balancing precariously on its point. In fact, huge effort is required just to prop it up, with people pushing hard (represented by the arrows), often in opposite directions. In the right pyramid, effort is invested in relationship development, which provides a stable structure in order to deliver the result. True results-oriented people prioritise the cultivation of relationships.

What does all this have to do with systems, and with delegation? The answer is that systems impinge on our delegation project through people. Systems can seem to be tyrannical, impersonal forces but apart from natural phenomena like earthquakes and weather events systems are the aggregate effects of human decisions, behaviours, words and deeds. Even remote and dis-embodied phenomena like the price of oil, which affects us all thanks to a densely interlinked global economy, results from the actions of men and women – from Opec ministers and oil futures traders, to presidents and consumers. System forces ripple along to us through the web of human relationships, which means it is possible to rebel against systems, or mitigate their effects, through the same medium – the web of human relationships.

Let's go back to Steve and Jason. A number of factors led to the delegation coming unstuck. A big one was Jason's sense of being oppressed by requirements that were beyond his ability to meet, such as precautions against acts of terrorism. That requirement was a system force originating in government regulations affecting ports, which rippled down to Jason from government through the Aberdeen Port Authority, down to the main contractor Bauen, and finally to Frank, Bauen's project manager, whose job it was to enforce the requirement and assess MT's compliance. In that sense, Frank and Jason together form the node where MT's system of systems intersect with Bauen's system of systems. But Frank was not happy. He was drumming his fingers, waiting for the terrorism risk assessment. Perturbed at MT's haphazard approach, Frank was losing confidence in MT's ability to do the job, with potentially bad consequences for MT. Had Steve listened to Jason, and paid attention to feedback from the systems, he would have realised this.

I said before that deep and deliberate delegation is no easy ride for the delegator. Much is required and pushing back against systems is another instance where the delegator must get involved. Since we respond to the tyranny of systems through relationships, Steve could have backed Jason up by working on the relevant relationships, in this case, with Frank. Steve could have provided what we might call relationship air cover with regard to Frank. As Jason's superior, Steve could have met with Frank, assured him that the terrorism precautions were a priority for MT, admitted that it was a little new for the company, requested some advice for complying, and asked for a bit more time. Thus reassured, and hopefully with some rapport established between himself and Steve, Frank would have had to be an abnormally stubborn or suspicious person not to offer some leeway, and even some help.

None of this is rocket science, but I am moved to explore it because, in our splintering organisational world, old-fashioned people skills are on the wane as electronic communications (text and email) encroach further into territory once reserved for face-to-face interactions. I've witnessed instances where a person tries to initiate an endeavour by sending an email and, when there is no response, or when the response is evasive, the matter is dropped. An entire avenue of endeavour is shut down with little more than, "Oh well, I tried". Email and text, as discussed in Chapter 14, are poor, low-bandwidth modes of communication. When people need to be persuaded, chivvied along, inspired, brought on board, or negotiated with, text and email are no substitute for deliberate, face-to-face encounters. I worry that we are beset by a new sense of fatalism, that we allow our conception of what is possible to be hemmed in by 'the way things are around here', which is really just the status quo of encroaching systems. Relationships offer a way of rebelling against their tyranny.

I've set out in this chapter how the successful result of a delegation requires a fresh and strategic approach to relationships (a relationships mindset, let's call it). That means all sorts of relationships: you both will need sponsors, allies, friends and helpers. But the most important relationship lies at the core of the delegation, you and the delegatee. This relationship, which is itself a system, needs to be big. I had hoped to introduce this idea to Steve and Jason, because their relationship was precarious. Sadly, though, with Jason's resignation, that opportunity was lost.

Or was it?

Chapter 19 Reflections, ideas and tools

Reflection • Think about a person whose indifference might stand in the way of your Courageous delegation outcome. What if you got the chance to speak to them, and interest them in the outcome? What would you say?

Idea • System forces ripple along to us through the medium of people: what they think, what they say, and what they do. So, the best way to mount a response to system forces is through relationships: the right relationships with the right people.

Tool • Use the map you drew of your systems (Chapter 18 tools) to identify the strategic relationships most in need of cultivation and development.

BIG RELATIONSHIPS, BIG RESULTS

"[E]verything in the world is connected and … it is the relationship between things rather than the things themselves that is the primary determinant of desirable or undesirable outcomes"

— John Blakey and Ian Day

On the Monday, to everyone's surprise and relief, Jason withdrew his resignation. He'd mulled over Steve's offer, decided that it was sincere, and that it was a valuable opportunity. No one was more relieved than Steve, on whose watch the crisis had unfolded, putting an important project for MT at risk and creating for himself a major problem to solve. Rob, the managing director, asked me to work with Steve and Jason to help them operate better together as a delegation team. It was to be a pilot development exercise that could perhaps be replicated across the company. Naturally, I was eager to help.

Steve was of a generation for whom it didn't come naturally to talk about relationships but the two of them were basking in the glow of the salvaged situation, so he was happy to go along. I proposed the idea that, as delegator in an important delegation, Steve could help Jason by providing air cover by cultivating the right relationships, and he readily agreed. I then introduced the notion that big results required big relationships, and that the relationship between delegator and delegatee had to be big, as did other core relationships in the delegation project.

"Of course," said Steve confidently.

"Excellent," I said. "So, what is a 'big' relationship? Can the two of you work up a definition so we know what we're talking about?"

While they talked, I jotted things down on the flip chart and after a few minutes we settled on four characteristics that make a relationship big. They were: 1) mutual trust, 2) commitment, 3) honesty, and 4) communication.

"So, Steve, would you say yours and Jason's relationship is 'big' in that way?" I asked.

"Absolutely," Steve said, growing a little less sure.

"Come on Steve," Jason said, "we're at each other's throats half the time."

I suggested we dig a little deeper into each of the ingredients of a big relationship and, after a short discussion, we had working definitions for those. They were as follows:

- *Mutual trust:* We know the other will help, not undermine, progress toward the common goal.
- *Commitment:* We each do all we can to further the common goal.
- *Honesty:* We tell the truth about what's happening, and we are honest with ourselves about what we are doing and why.
- *Communication:* We give each other all necessary information when it is needed; we conceal nothing.

With those definitions before us in writing, Steve admitted that the relationship between him and Jason needed work.

Then I explained that, as a coach, I worked with healthy, coping adults, and believed that they were fine as they are. Years ago, as a manager, I used to try and fix people with amateur psychology, which of course never worked and often backfired. Now I subscribed to the view put forward by John Blakey and Ian Day in their book, *Challenging Coaching*, that 'everything in the world is connected and that it is the relationship between things rather than the things themselves that is the primary determinant of desirable or undesirable outcomes'.

The relationship between Steve and Jason is a system, I said, and they needed to understand it in order to make sure it was working properly.

The co-created pattern

To that end, looking back over the two years since Steve had come to Dundee, I asked them to describe how they tended to interact. At first, they were hesitant, but then the conversation got heated as they each remembered times when there was friction. I asked them to try and avoid arguing their cases all over again, but rather to think of themselves as impartial observers, recalling particularly what was said, and what was said in response. This interested them, and they talked keenly while I wrote down what was being said on the flip chart. After a quarter of an hour or so I asked them to stop and help me make sense of what I'd written. Grouping the statements into the most common themes, I wrote a condensed list on a fresh page. It looked like this:

Steve:

This needs to be done …

Why isn't it done?

When will you do it?

I told you last month …

That's no excuse …

Jason:

I need more time …

I'm doing my best …

You never explained …

Look at the hours I'm putting in …

You don't understand …

Then I asked them how an impartial outsider might sum up or label their respective lists of statements, in just one or two words. After some hemming and hawing, Steve allowed the words 'demanding' and 'blaming', and Jason agreed to 'self-justifying' and 'pleading'.

"Okay, thanks," I said. "Now, what do you notice about your typical statements?"

"We're just going back and forth," Jason said.

"Yes, I'm glad you said that, because that's how it seems to me," I said.

That allowed me to propose to them the idea of the co-created pattern, which, I explained, was a self-reinforcing cycle of behaviour between two people that can arise in times of strain, and which limits each person's freedom to respond in novel, productive ways. In this case the co-created pattern could be expressed as 'the more Steve blames and demands, the more Jason self-justifies and pleads, and the more Jason does that, the more Steve blames and demands'.

They stiffened, but did not object.

"It's important to remember," I said, "that we are not interested in who started it, or whose fault it is. There are no 'rights' and 'wrongs'. It's just the way it is. We're probing the possibility that each response stimulates more of the same from the other, and two individuals can sometimes get stuck in a pattern that fuels itself and undermines the relationship by clouding it with hostility, suspicion and passive aggression. Communication is mostly defensive. Trust, honesty, commitment are weak."

They both agreed that this was possible.

Encouraged, I continued. "So, the question becomes, how to break the pattern?"

"Easy," said Jason. "Steve needs to stop being a miserable git."

"Yes," laughed Steve, "and Jason needs to stop being useless."

We all enjoyed the joke.

"Seriously, though," I said, "we know Steve is more than just a miserable git, and that Jason is far from useless. That means the conditions do exist for the relationship to be based on mutual trust, commitment, honesty and good communication, don't they?"

They agreed, and they also agreed that the current co-created pattern was not effective. On the flip chart I sketched it like this:

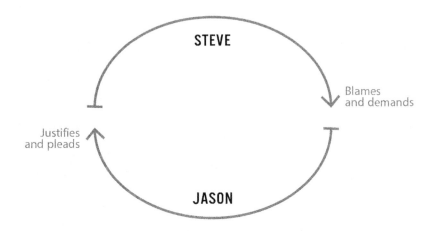

INEFFECTIVE **CO-CREATED PATTERN**

FIGURE 8. Ineffective Co-created Pattern (Credit: Dave Stitt)

To probe what such a relationship would look like, I introduced the concept of 'managing by requests and promises'.

Managing by requests and promises

If delegator and delegatee each accept that the other is trustworthy, committed, honest and willing to communicate, then an interesting possibility arises. They could stop viewing their relationship in terms of 'boss issues instructions to direct report', and to see it instead as peers needing things from each other in order to achieve their common goal. How would they behave in that circumstance? The concept of 'managing by requests and promises', also developed by Werner Erhard, was introduced to me by my first business coach, who also introduced me to the mysteries of the Results Pyramid.[17]

---

17   Some of the materials in this chapter, specifically 'Managing by requests and promises', are the property of Landmark Worlwide LLC and Werner Erhard, and are used with permission.

"It works like this," I said. "Let's say I'm the delegator. I request that you do something, and you have four responses to choose from." On a fresh page of the flip chart, I wrote the following:

"Yes."
"Yes, if …"
"Yes, but …"
"No."

I delved a little deeper into the four responses.

"Yes means yes," I said. "That becomes your promise, and you don't break it. If you do, your credibility suffers. 'Yes, if …' means yes with a condition. You need something from me in return, such as an essential bit of information, an introduction to someone, a decision, or help with something. 'Yes, but …' means yes, but with modifications, such as not by the time I want, or not exactly in the way I want. And 'No' means no, and it must be respected. Thoughts so far?"

"Looks like the tail wagging the dog, to me," said Steve.

"How so?" I said.

"He can just say no. How will anything get done?"

"Good question Steve," I said. "But you're assuming he would say 'no' without adequate reason. If you trust your delegatee, and he is as committed as you are to the common goal, and is honest and open, why would he tend to say 'no'?"

While Steve mulled that over, I explained more of the thinking behind the approach.

It assumes the request is not easy but, having thought it

through, you believe the action is necessary to the common goal. Furthermore, you assume the delegatee can do it. Because the two of you communicate at a high level you can set out your reasoning and expect an honest and considered response. If you've chosen the request well, the delegatee's response might be: "Yikes, I'm not sure how I'm going to do that, but I have some ideas and I think I know who might be able to help, so, yes, leave it to me." You trust him to get on with it and report back if there is an issue. On the other hand, you may not have a completely accurate picture of the terrain and the delegatee responds with 'Yes, if' or 'Yes, but'. A conversation ensues, eliciting good feedback from the task, and from systems, followed by a negotiation in which the delegatee asks for support. Having agreed to those requests, you must deliver on your side of the bargain. These counter-requests may be stretching in themselves. Both delegator and delegatee take on "big" accountability.

"This goes against the grain for us, Steve, because we were trained to give instructions," I said. "However, when you give someone an instruction you are imposing your authority, and sometimes bosses need to do that, but if it is your only way of managing you may find that you're forever being a policeman, checking up on people, and also regularly being let down and frustrated by excuses. Managing by requests and promises allows stronger and more reliable bonds between people and to the common goal.

"If the delegatee says 'No'," I said, "that must be respected, but the reasons must be intelligible. If it happens regularly it means there is an issue, such as a misalignment between your and his expectations and levels of commitment."

The request-and-promise ethic is meant to stretch and empower individuals. It requires high levels of mutual trust, commitment, honesty and communication, but when it takes root in an organisation, the organisation and everyone in it stretches. I've been lucky enough to see it in action for periods of time in the top management levels of companies and, as a result, the companies became 'supercharged'. It is difficult to make such a state permanent among the top tiers of management because it is a rare and delicate dynamic. It takes only one person or one clique to revert to less-than-honest, self-aggrandising or passive aggressive patterns of behaviour for the whole thing to deflate, and for people to seek safety again in routines and strict adherence to job descriptions. For smaller teams, though, which are the relevant 'units' when it comes to delegation, the request-and-promise ethic can be built quickly and sustained more easily. Such teams often become hotspots of capability and innovation in larger organisations.

I stopped to let that all sink in. Jason was beaming.

"Phew," said Steve. "I'm going to have to get my act together."

"You both will," I said, explaining that we have to make efforts and break habits to maintain an awareness of systems and cultivate strategic relationships. We don't master a new skill by having it accurately described to us; it takes practice, trial and error. They looked interested, so I asked: "If you shifted the pattern between you to be more effective, what would it look like?" This is what they came up with, and each committed to make a start and notice and acknowledge each other's positive actions toward the shift.

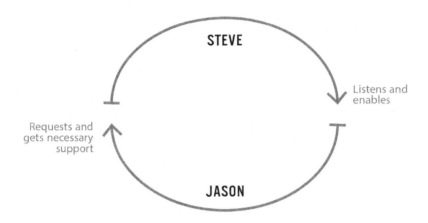

EFFECTIVE **CO-CREATED PATTERN**

FIGURE 9. Effective Co-Created Pattern (Credit: Dave Stitt)

We have almost come to the end. The time has come to bring it all together, and to ask a provocative question. The point of this book is to help you unleash talent in your team or organisation, and to win back time: but time to do what?

Chapter 20 Reflections, ideas and tools

Idea • Big results require big relationships between you and the delegatee and among others the outcome relies upon. Big relationships are characterised by 1) mutual trust, 2) commitment, 3) honesty, and 4) communication.

Reflection • What situations that your team encounters call for big relationships? If you can't think of any you may be coasting, stuck in routine, governed by the status quo.

Idea • Ineffective co-created patterns are cycles of mutually reinforcing counterproductive responses. Disrupt them and turn them into effective, positive co-created patterns.

Tool • Manage by requests and promises: Ask something big and allow the other to say no.

CONCLUSION
BRINGING IT ALL TOGETHER

In the last chapter, Steve felt overwhelmed by all he needed to think about, and do, in order to cultivate big relationships. "I'm going to have to get my act together," he'd said. Maybe you're feeling overwhelmed, too, by that and by all that's involved with deep and deliberate delegation. You may be thinking, hang on, I thought this was supposed to unleash talent and *win back time*? It sounds very *time-consuming*!

It's natural to feel this way. Remember, we're cracking open the pebble of the old, worn-down concept of delegation, refurbishing and expanding its constituent parts, and putting them back together again. For many it will all be new. Old habits of thought and action will need to be unlearned but, over a short period of time and with practice, the new habits of deep and deliberate delegation will form and become second nature, allowing you to reap the harvest of talent and time. And it will be contagious. When you practice deep and deliberate delegation, you teach it to the delegatee, who in turn passes the *modus operandi* on, enabling ground-up culture change. It is the natural subversion of the status quo, the *guerrilla*-style restoration of purpose and engagement, of accountability and capability.

We started with the feeling of being stuck, of your team, department or organisation being oppressed by limits, constrained by the status quo, which you and others in the organisation have collectively, unconsciously accepted. Think of the organisation as being water, frozen in a pot. You and the other individuals are the water molecules and you are packed together, barely moving. Deep and deliberate delegation is like heat, which sets those molecules vibrating. When the heat is applied, the ice starts to melt and the movement of molecules speeds up and spreads. Keep applying the heat and before long the water is boiling.

Let's recap.

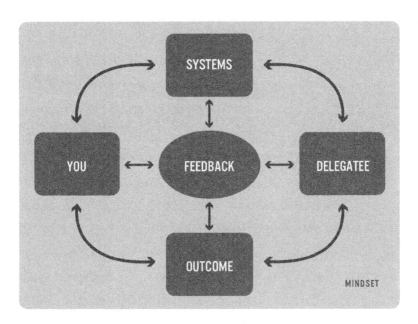

FIGURE 1. The dynamic of deep and deliberate delegation (Credit: Dave Stitt)

You, the delegator

The first constituent part of deep and deliberate delegation is you and, if you are reading this book, chances are you are feeling stuck. That's not a bad thing. Remember that the feeling of being stuck is the tension between what is and what could be, so it is also an opportunity. The feeling of being stuck arises in leaders of teams and organisations who have lost traction. They have hit the limit of what they can do and their influence has become weakened and buried under the organisational status quo. They need to become sticky again, meaning they are able to lure people out of their grooves and enlist them in new, important endeavours.

The deep and deliberate delegator understands that to enlist a helper for something important the delegator must break off a chunk of her accountability and pass it in a managed way to the delegatee. But what? A good decision about what to give away requires you to look afresh at what it is only you should be doing, and there are two places to look for that. The first is your Zone of Mastery, or Unique Ability, the zone you inhabit when you're doing what you love most, what only you can do, and where the results are remarkable. However, since this is your work or professional life, you need to apply a second filter, which is the field of activity most necessary to get your organisation heading in the direction it needs to go. Where those two filters overlap, that's what you should be doing. All accountabilities falling outside those boundaries are ripe for delegation, which will win you time.

The delegatee

The alchemy of delegation begins with the activation of the delegatee. This is where talent is unleashed because deep and deliberate delegation is a powerful motivator and enabler. It gives your employees the chance to develop mastery, autonomy and purpose, and to grow in confidence and capability. However, many would-be delegators get stuck at this point, which is a big reason why they feel stuck in the broader sense. The problem is, how can you suddenly trust your delegatee with something big when you didn't before?

While it would be nice to have super-resourceful and proven people on hand when we need to achieve a result – James Bond, say – the fact is, we have who we have. What's more, in many reluctant delegators I encounter a big overhang of pessimism regarding would-be delegatees. Deep and deliberate delegation does not require you to have blind faith in people you believe are not up to the job, but are they really not up to the job? Often the stance of mistrust adopted by bosses is reflexive, and it can be an excuse not to try delegating, to stay in one's uncomfortable comfort zone.

The philosopher Onora O'Neill can help us break the trust logjam by moving the focus away from trust, which is a feeling we either have or do not have, and on to trustworthiness, which is a trait the other person has or does not have. The mindset of deep and deliberate delegation requires you to be curious about the trustworthiness of your potential delegatees. Use the Trustworthy Tracker to assess their trustworthiness based on evidence. It will help you select the right person to delegate to, and to start working with who you've got. If you conclude that there is simply nobody you can trust with a delegated outcome, there are questions to be asked about your recruitment process.

You are surrounded by people and each one of those people has talents and resources you can only guess at. You can't know all they're capable of because now their role is defined and limited by the status quo. They could help you, but they don't, because they don't know you're stuck. You haven't told them, or asked for their help. If you're still inclined to pigeon-hole people based on gut feeling, remember Laura Dekker, who sailed solo around the world at sixteen. Remember also to cultivate a growth mindset as described by Carol Dweck, which sees ability as something that can be developed through effort and practice, and challenge a fixed mindset, which asserts that people are born with a certain amount of brains and talent and nothing they can do will change that.

The thing that is delegated

You're going to begin passing accountabilities over to your delegatees, but what form will this take? There are three categories of delegated things ranging in their impact (in terms of unleashing talent and winning back time) from modest, to intermediate, to big. At the modest end of the scale you delegate a task, the one-off job. At the intermediate level, you delegate a process, where your delegatee takes over the running of something. And at the big end, you delegate an outcome. Going over this in some more detail, recall that tasks are entry-level delegation, baby steps, a place to start; when the task is finished you're back to square one. Delegating a process frees up far more of your time, but if process delegation is just a promotion it can leave the status quo unchallenged. Outcome delegation is the most liberating for you and the most stretching for the delegatee. You're asking the delegatee to accomplish something big that falls outside current processes or even cut across them, thus disrupting the status quo.

How you conceive and articulate the delegation outcome matters a great deal. You are selling a new reality and offering the delegatee a role in making it happen. To secure her commitment and enthusiasm, the vision must be exciting and vivid but also intelligible and detailed. This is you being sticky and the delegation outcome as an idea must also be sticky, as Chip and Dan Heath have set out. This calls for clarity of thought and precision in language. The familiar goal-setting technique of SMART is a basic necessity but for more ambitious delegations 'Courageous' goal-setting is required.

Having articulated the delegation outcome and secured the delegatee's buy-in you must let go, and not be a sneaky micromanager. There are many ways a delegator can seem to let go while maintaining a stealthy grip on the outcome. For instance, resist the temptation to construct a solution to the problem that seems to match the problem in its scale and detail; that is a way of trying to maintain control. You want the delegatee to become a new outpost of independent, dynamic capability, to unleash her talent, so empower her to find her own way through. Remember Jerry and Monique Sternin and the malnourished children in Vietnam? They couldn't have designed a solution to that problem, but they knew the solution was there among the people themselves. Instead of asking, "What is the problem and how can we fix it?", they asked, "What is working around here and how can we do more of it?" Let the delegatee investigate that latter question.

The art of feedback

You will let the delegatee get on with it, but you will not abandon her. You must still be involved, but as a supporter and challenger, not as a puppeteer. She is now accountable for calling into being a new reality and feedback is what nurtures the successful realisation of that accountability. Feedback is the pipe through which flow the nutrients of encouragement, advice, challenge and support from you to her, and back through which flow to you both essential intelligence about the endeavour. This requires big conversations that hold the delegatee to account, but in a way that builds mutual trust and confidence.

Few of us emerge into working life fully equipped to give and receive such feedback. We tend to avoid awkward conversations with friends and colleagues, so it is even more difficult to have such conversations with people we barely know. The Delegation Feedback Conversation provides a framework for covering all the necessary ground, including: setting milestones; assessing progress; identifying problems and strategies for overcoming them; and offering help.

Feedback cannot always be nice, however. If the endeavour is at all ambitious, the delegatee will be put to the test and will need to be challenged to raise her game. Higher challenge must be balanced with higher support, though. Too much challenge leads to stress, blame and risk aversion, while too much support leads to smug complacency and slipping standards. Deliberate feedback requires the delegator to raise his game, showing extra skill, consideration and commitment.

There is another element to feedback beyond communication between the two of you. Feedback must also be actively sought from the endeavour itself, and from the environment you're working in, which leads us to systems.

Systems and all that gets in the way

If we operated in laboratory conditions, deep and deliberate delegation would be simple, but we operate in the world, and the world will mess with you. Through systems, the world interferes. Systems are forces that we cannot see or touch. They can be financial, personal, social, physical, cultural, economic, political, technological and more. The influence we have over them is weak and gets weaker the farther out from our own little worlds we look. But it doesn't work the other way around, for systems we cannot control have no trouble reaching in to meddle with us, such as when a strike by air traffic controllers cancels my flight home, or the collapse in the price of oil ruins my business.

You can mount a response to systems in order to protect your delegation outcome, but first you and your delegatee need to be aware of systems, something surprisingly few of us even think about. Try understanding systems better by noticing and describing their influence in the following seven zones, starting with the immediate and working out to the global: 1) your physical work environment; 2) your work culture; 3) the relationships that matter; 4) your organisation and its customers; 5) your sector; 6) the national view; 7) the global view. Developing a systems perspective is liberating because it allows you to avoid blaming failure on individuals, or on other single events or elements.

Remember, it is not the things themselves that are most important but rather the relationships between things.

Because system forces ripple along to us through the medium of people, the best way to rebel against the tyranny of systems is through relationships: we need the right relationships with the right people, and one way you can support your delegatee in achieving the delegation outcome is by providing relationship air cover. For instance, if your delegatee's way is being blocked by someone senior in another department on some bureaucratic pretext or other, it might help if you sat down with that person to explain what you're trying to achieve. Try using your new-found stickiness to sell the vision more broadly.

A systems perspective leads us to a simple, profound insight: that results flow most reliably not from action but from relationships. Action-oriented people can fall into the trap of thinking that achieving great things depends on working harder and faster, on being stronger and more determined than everyone else, when actually a quiet chat with the right person can do the trick.

The most important relationship in the delegation is between you and your delegatee and, in order to achieve big results, that relationship and other core relationships in the delegation need to be big, that is, characterised by mutual trust, commitment, honesty, and communication.

What will you do with your time?

To explore deep and deliberate delegation throughout this book I've concentrated on a single delegation endeavour between you and the delegatee, but that shouldn't be taken to mean that a single delegation endeavour is necessarily enough to unleash talent and win back time. This is to get you started on the project of spending as much time in your Zone of Mastery as possible. As the approach outlined here becomes second nature you may have several different delegation endeavours going on at once and at different stages. Ideally, your delegatees will become delegators in their own right, too, causing a culture of deep and deliberate delegation to spread like heat in the organisation.

Now we turn to the question I want to leave you with: what will you do with the time you win back? The biggest complaint among the executives I work with is that there is not enough time in the day. They feel stuck, and see themselves as constrained by a lack of time. Most of them have been on time management courses, as have I, but they still don't have enough time. One senior director I know went on a two-day time management course and was so busy on his return catching up with issues that he never got around to reading the literature or trying the techniques. Several years on, he is still catching up.

Time management strategies tend to revolve around prioritising what you think you have to do and practising various techniques for sticking to those priorities. But it is no panacea because things just take as long as they take. Assuming that you are a seasoned practitioner, a piece of work – whether it is tilling a field, researching a market, chairing a meeting, writing a report, holding a deliberate conversation, conducting a negotiation – will take as long as it takes. Sometimes a new technology will come along that dramatically shortens a task or eliminates the need for it altogether but, generally, there are no short cuts to the correct attainment of a quality result.

In that sense, time cannot be managed. It cannot be tamed,

or improved, or cajoled, or negotiated with. It is a finite, precious resource that pays no attention to you. There are twenty-four hours in a day and that is that. The idea that a top-flight executive can finely mince time – spending eleven minutes on a penetrating analysis here, and fourteen minutes negotiating a breakthrough deal there – is farfetched. If you are a terrible procrastinator, or are pathologically distractible, then yes, learn some time management techniques. But if you are diligent to a normal degree already you cannot really manage time, you can only give it away by doing more or win it back by doing less, which is what delegation does.

But what will you do with the time you win back? I suspect that in our heart of hearts many of us shrink from the question. Commentators have noticed that sometimes we seem to be busy for the sake of it, perhaps to appear indispensable, because we worry that if we are not frantically racing around someone might question our fundamental usefulness. 'Busyness,' wrote the essayist Tim Kreider in the *New York Times*,[18] 'serves as a kind of existential reassurance, a hedge against emptiness; obviously your life cannot possibly be silly or trivial or meaningless if you are so busy, completely booked, in demand every hour of the day.'

That's harsh, but among the executives I coach, I do sense unease with a more practical sort of question, which might be expressed as, "If I mastered the art of delegation, and relieved myself of the burden of doing everything, of constantly fighting fires, and of intervening in others' work and 'improving' it, what

---

18   "The Busy Trap", *New York Times*, June 30, 2012. https://opinionator.blogs.nytimes.com/2012/06/30/the-busy-trap/

actually would I do with my days?"

We come to the nub of the issue. If you are in charge of a team, a department or a company, as captain of the ship your real job is not to be down among the crew, immersed in their processes, but instead to be up on the bridge working out where the ship should be heading. When my clients complain about not having enough time what they worry about most is their chronic neglect of strategic thinking.

From what I've observed over many years as a coach to executive boards, this is endemic among organisations. What do we want our team or organisation to be doing in one, three, five years' time? What sort of customers should we have? How will we stand out? What will people be saying about us? These are basic questions that many leaders cannot begin to answer. The problem is, it requires down time to work out an answer. You have to be un-busy, idle; you need to spend time thinking, daydreaming, reading, talking to people, playing with ideas, and who has time for that?

Deep and deliberate delegation, as well as unleashing talent in your organisation, does what time management cannot do: it gives you time, time not only to leave work behind and enjoy your life, but also to do the higher-level work of setting a strategic course. I call it higher-level work because it is at this level that you can make the biggest difference.

What to do now?

We do not master an art by having it accurately described to us. This book is a distillation of a number of programmes I deliver on deep and deliberate delegation, which provide an immersive approach to exploring and practising the ideas and techniques explored here. To find out more about mastering the art and promoting it in your organisation, visit:

www.DaveStitt.com

Acknowledgements

I have many to thank for this book. First, I owe special acknowledgment to Mark Thompson for alerting me to the importance of delegation and for providing a test bed for the techniques described here. Big thanks also go to my wife Sue for her belief in me and for inspiring me to press on. For their generous help with insights and advice on initial drafts, I am extremely grateful to Mark and Sue, and also to Luis Amorim, John Blakey, Andy Bull, Ian Cuthbertson, Susan Dawson, Phil Dixon, Jocelyn Gill, Chris Godfrey, John Merriman and Alison Whybrow. For helping me to put flesh on the bones and pull it all together, I'm grateful to my editor, Rod Sweet. Results do indeed flow from relationships.

INDEX OF REFLECTIONS, IDEAS AND TOOLS

Reflection • Take ten minutes and allow yourself to daydream about the things that should be happening but are not happening. Write them down. Now, pick the most important. Imagine it happening. Who is doing it? Who notices? Who is affected, and how?

Idea • The feeling of being stuck is the tension between what is and what could be. It is a growing knot of concerns and half-formed ideas. People can help but right now those people, with all their talents and resources, are just sliding by. *(page 17)*

Idea • To stop being a Custodian of the Status Quo and become instead an Agent of Change, you need to become "sticky", meaning people want to be part of your plan and will put their resources to work for it. You need to shake up settled processes and lure people out of their grooves. To start with, one person will do. *(page 18)*

Idea • Good delegators:

Reflection • Who do you know that delegates really well? Do they do all five of the above? Do they do other things as well? Which of the above do you already do, and which would you like to improve?

Chapter 3. Do what you want to do (page 28)

Reflection • What is your **Unique Ability?** When were you last in your Zone of Mastery, and what were you doing? You are in your Zone of Mastery when 1) people admire you because the results are stunning; 2) you love doing it and time flies; 3) it gives you energy rather than sapping it; and 4) you get better at it all the time. *(page 32)*

Idea • Tasks and responsibilities that eat up lots of time and fall farthest from your Zone of Mastery are ripest for delegation. *(page 36)*

Tool • The **Time Tracker**: Do an audit on how you actually spend your working week. Set your phone or watch to beep every hour during your working day for two or three weeks, and jot down whatever you're doing at that moment. Map those onto the Bullseye of Mastery chart to see how much time you spend in the zones of Rank Incompetence, Dreary Competence, Passionless Skill and Mastery. *(page 37)*

Chapter 4. Do what is really necessary (page 39)

Idea • Being leader of a team, department or organisation should not mean you are Chief Problem Solver. If you are, you are working one or two pay grades below what you were hired to do. *(page 40)*

Idea • Your real job is to conceive and articulate a vision for where your team, department or organisation should be heading, and, with help from your people, to work out a detailed roadmap (strategy) for how to get there. *(pages 40-41)*

Reflection • Ask yourself and others what things you can do that will get your 'ship' moving toward the vision, and what among those things fall inside your Zone of Mastery.

Reflection • Uncommon results require uncommon motivation. What signs of motivation or de-motivation do you detect in your team?

Idea • The most powerful motivators are "intrinsic": they arise out of the work itself. But still we rely most on "extrinsic" motivators such as pay or perks. *(pages 49-50)*

Idea • People find work intrinsically motivating when it bestows 1) autonomy, 2) mastery and 3) purpose. Deep and deliberate delegation promotes all three. *(pages 50-54)*

Tool • Further reading: *Drive: The Surprising Truth About What Motivates Us*, by Daniel Pink. Canongate, 2010.

Reflection • Delegators can sometimes be paralysed by a reflexive pessimism toward their potential delegatees. Are you? Think of the people around you that you trust the least and jot down why.

Idea • The young person in front of you is every bit as intelligent and committed as you were when you began. *(page 57-58)*

Idea • Demonstrable trustworthiness should be the focus, not the subjective feeling of trust. *(pages 59-60)*

Tool • Use the **Trustworthy Tracker** to query your pessimism by assessing the potential delegatee's trustworthiness on four metrics: 1) Caring, 2) Honest, 3) Reliable and 4) Competent. *(page 63)*

Chapter 7. Mindset: mental habits that will help you both (page 69)
Reflection • Check and challenge the "map" you've made of your candidate delegatee. Do you really know what is going on for him and why he behaves as he does? What if you asked him? *(page 69)*

Idea • If you pigeon-hole people, you will probably get it wrong: **remember Laura Dekker**, who sailed solo around the world at sixteen. *(pages 71-72)*

Idea • People with a **growth mindset** see their ability as something they can develop through effort, learning and practice, while people with a **fixed mindset** believe they were born with a finite amount of brains and talent. Thanks to Carol Dweck for that insight. *(page 73)*

Reflection • Nobody likes to admit to having a **fixed mindset**, so watch yourself and your team for fixed mindset statements:

"We've just got to get through this week." "Our people are too inexperienced." "There's not enough time." "It's down to personality." "It didn't work, so..." "They just have the wrong attitude." "It all boils down to just one thing…"

Tool • Further reading: Mindset: *The New Psychology of Success*, Carol S. Dweck, Random House, 2006.

Part Three: The thing that is delegated *(page 79)*
Chapter 8. Tasks, processes and outcomes (page 81)
Reflection • To win back time and unleash talent you have to **delegate something substantial**. You can tell if the delegated thing is substantial if: 1) It hurts a bit to give up; 2) It feels risky to let go; 3) It is stretching for the delegatee; 4) It makes you all a bit nervous; and 4) It constitutes a good chunk of your time, 20% for example, based on your Time Tracker results, from Chapter 3. *(page 82)*

Idea • There are three levels of delegated things: **Tasks**, **Processes** and **Outcomes**. Tasks are one-off jobs: entry-level delegation. Processes are ongoing operational functions. Outcomes are more challenging, and may disrupt processes, offering the most opportunity for freedom and growth. *(page 83)*

Reflection • Stop and think about all that needs to be happening but isn't. If you could delegate one process or outcome that would make a big difference, what would it be?

Tool • If you really don't know what you should delegate, ask trusted colleagues. They are bound to have some ideas! *(page 81)*

Chapter 9. How to define it, and get buy in (page 89)

Reflection • The "A" in SMART is for "agreed". Visualise what the delegatee will look like, what his demeanour will be, when he agrees. There should be some excitement, some back and forth conversation between the two of you as you explore together the specifics and ramifications. There may be some negotiating. Now picture him sitting in front of you, nodding simply to keep you happy and bring the conversation to an end.

Tool • Apply the "Specific Test" to your language. It goes like this: 1) Somebody must do something he or she was not doing before. 2) The "do" is a good, ordinary verb that a child will understand. If you are not sure, find a child and ask him if he understands the verb. 3) Doing the thing will have a tangible result, one that we want. (Watch out for weak, weaselly, abstract verbs like "optimise", "review", "oversee" and "support".) *(page 92)*

Tool • Ask the delegatee to summarise the delegation back to you and listen carefully to the words he uses. Are they specific, and is his specific the same as your specific? Challenge the non-committal words like "hope" and "try"; get beneath the surface of his reservations so you can work through them. *(page 95)*

Chapter 10. Why it pays to be Courageous (page 97)

Reflection • Think of a desirable but "unrealistic" outcome. Why exactly it is unrealistic? Whose comfort zones does it disrupt?

Idea • Courageous goals have their own momentum. They

force a change of scene, raise entirely new questions, and call new relationships into being. They also ward off the effects of "enthusiasm half-life". *(pages 101-103)*

Tool • Use the **Courageous Goal Starter Kit** to get things moving: 1) Dream it, 2) Declare it, and 3) Get started. *(page 100)*

Tool • Make the story **"sticky" with SUCCES**: Get more buy-in for your Courageous outcome by describing it using the principles defined by Chip and Dan Heath and their acronym, SUCCES – it should be 1) Simple, 2) Unexpected, 3) Concrete, 4) Credible, 5) Emotional, and 6) contain a Story. *(pages 103-105)*

Chapter 11. Why you must really let go, and how to do it (page 109)
Reflection • Think of the Courageous outcome you want. Is it more difficult than the Sternin's challenge of solving **child malnutrition in Vietnam?** *(pages 109-113)*

Idea • An ambitious delegation is **complex, not complicated**, which means you cannot devise in advance a fool proof plan for achieving it. Like the Sternins' approach to tackling child malnutrition in Vietnam, you will need to really let go, and support the delegatee as he feels his way along, seeking the necessary wisdom and capability that is already there, latent and concealed in the systems. *(pages 113-115)*

Idea • Achieving complex outcomes requires us to avoid the **trap of situational symmetry**, meaning our urge, when faced with a complex problem, to try and design a solution that seems equal to the problem in scale and detail. *(pages 115-116)*

Tool • Harness the **power of Positive Deviance**: Do not ask "What is the problem and how can we fix it?" Instead, ask "What is working around here, and how can we do more of it?" *(pages 117-118)*

Tool • **Value progress**, and do not be **paralysed by perfection**: cultivate your confidence by focussing on the distance travelled from the beginning, not on the distance remaining to the end. (Thanks for the insight, Dan Sullivan!) *(pages 117-118)*

Part Four: The art of feedback *(page 121)*

Chapter 12. True feedback needs true accountability (page 123)

Reflection • If you had to hold three awkward but productive conversations tomorrow, who would they be with, and what would they be about? Would you be equipped to hold them?

Idea • Without effective goal setting there can be no holding to account and, therefore, no accountability. **If there is no accountability, feedback is meaningless**. It will lack purpose and be arbitrary. At worst, it is the mere projection onto an employee of the boss's own issues. So, deal with goal-setting and accountability first. *(pages 125-127)*

Idea • Where there is no true accountability, off-the-shelf annual appraisals anger and alienate employees because they impose a template for an idealised employee with a checklist of traits, competencies and behaviours that may have no relevance to the employee or her actual job. *(page 128)*

Tool • Try forgetting about a person's weaknesses and instead

praise and deploy their strengths. Improving weaknesses only leads to stronger weaknesses: in other words, mediocrity. *(page 129-130)*

Idea • Deep and deliberate delegation bestows genuine accountability. As such, it is the *guerrilla*-style, ground-up restoration of purpose and engagement in work. *(page 131)*

Chapter 13. Setting the scene for big conversations (page 133)
Reflection • Think about your own conversational style. In what ways might it get in the way of holding productive conversations?

Idea • With delegation you give up hard control and replace it with something more subtle: influence. But don't underestimate the power of influence. The delegatee still needs you. She needs advice and encouragement in order to have confidence and make good decisions in the field. She will also need to be challenged and corrected from time to time, because none of us are infallible. This is feedback. *(pages 136-137)*

Idea • Feedback needs a medium – a pipe – and that medium is conversation. The Delegation Feedback Conversation needs to be "big" because it has important jobs to do. In it, progress is reported and assessed, barriers are identified, strategies are devised, the delegatee is encouraged and challenged, and the delegator commits to help. *(pages 136-137)*

Idea • Few of us emerge into working life naturally equipped to hold such a conversation. *(pages 136-139)*

Chapter 14. How to conduct a Delegation Feedback Conversation (page 141)

Tool • The Delegation Feedback Conversation *(pages 142-145)*

1. Pick the five most important milestones needed to move the delegation forward right now.

2. Have the delegatee rate progress on the first milestone with a score of zero to ten.

3. Ask the delegatee, "What is the main reason for your score?" Listen, make notes.

4. Then ask the delegatee, "What would need to have happened for you to score a ten?" Listen and make notes.

5. When all five milestones have been scored and discussed, average the scores to get the delegatee's "Happy Score". Record this to track progress.

6. Review notes and reset the milestones five new ones, to be scored at the next Feedback Conversation.

7. Encourage the delegatee, and agree on how you will help with the new milestones.

Tool • **The DOS conversation**: If the delegatee is paralysed by emotion, reset the milestones by exploring Dangers, Opportunities and Strengths. *(page 146)*

Tool • **The Stockdale Paradox**: If morale is really suffering, reset milestones by facing brutal facts. *(page 148)*

Chapter 15. When, and how, to get tough (page 153)

Reflection • What difficult conversation do you need to have but have been putting off because you don't want to upset the other person?

Idea • An ambitious delegation requires you to give lots of both support and challenge to the delegatee See Blakey's and Day's **Support Challenge Matrix** for how this works. *(page 154)*

Idea • Too much challenge is the zone of stress, burn-out and uneven results. Too much support is the zone of complacency and slipping standards. Too little of each is the zone of inertia, apathy, isolation and boredom. *(page 155)*

Tool • Further reading: *Challenging Coaching*, by John Blakey and Ian Day (Nicholas Brealy Publishing, 2012)

Chapter 16. Seven more tips on delegation feedback (page 163)
Tools • Seven more tips on delegation feedback:
1. Feed back often, good and bad: Get into the habit of providing feedback regularly, so you and the delegatee get used to it. *(page 164)*
2. You are on the same team: Check your feedback style and assumptions. Are you being adversarial or collaborative? *(page 165)*
3. Address the method, not the madness: Don't use feedback to try and 'fix' aspects of the delegatee's character. That attacks a person's sense of self worth. Stick to tactics, knowledge, tips, and work routines. *(page 166)*
4. Disrupt patterns of generalities: Vague and evasive language can undermine feedback; learn to spot and challenge it. *(page 167)*
5. Offer suggestions instead of criticising: Instead of using the

feedback sandwich to sweeten criticism, make a suggestion and offer two reasons why it might work. *(page 168)*

6. Listen actively: Prove you are listening; Reserve judgement until everything has been said; Focus on what's being said, not how you're feeling about it. *(page 171)*

7. Everything is feedback: You're always communicating so to take control and give the feedback you have chosen to give. *(page 172)*

Part Five: Systems and all that gets in the way *(page 175)*

Chapter 17. How the world will mess with you (page 177)

Reflection • What caused Jason to resign? Poor communication? Bad management? Company over-reach? A lack of support? His own lack of experience? When no single factor seems to be an adequate explanation it is time to start paying attention to systems.

Idea • Delegation never happens in a vacuum; through systems the world will interfere. Systems are interlinked networks of forces that impinge on our puny zones of influence. They can be political, economic, social, environmental, technological or even internal and psychological. They include our physical surroundings and the culture and behaviours of our customers. *(pages 177-178)*

Idea • The influence we exert over systems weakens quickly the farther out we go from our zones of influence. It doesn't work the other way around, though, because systems over which we have no control can have a major impact on us, and on our delegation.

Idea • If we're not aware of systems, they can ambush us.

Chapter 18. What just happened? Mapping systems (page 185)
Reflection • Have you ever asked yourself, "Why is it so hard to get anything done around here?" A systems perspective avoids the trap of always attributing failure to particular individuals, or other single events or elements.

Idea • Getting feedback from systems helps you respond to their influence and protect the outcome of your delegation.

Tool • Understand systems better by interrogating their influence through the **Seven System Lenses**. They are: 1) Your physical work environment; 2) Your work culture; 3) The relationships that matter; 4) Your organisation and its customers; 5) Your sector; 6) The national view; 7) The global view. *(pages 188-196)*

Tool • **Map your systems:** This is a way for you and the delegatee to map the systems that are influencing your delegation, so you can both gain a better understanding of what is going on. *(pages 198-200)*

Tool • See, Systemic Coaching & Constellations, by John Whittington *(2nd ed., 2016)*

Chapter 19. Rebel against the tyranny of systems through relationships (page 201)

Reflection • Think about a person whose indifference might stand in the way of your Courageous delegation outcome. What if you got the chance to speak to them, and interest them in the outcome? What would you say?

Idea • Results flow best from relationships, not actions. Consider the **Results Pyramid**. *(page 203)*

Idea • System forces ripple along to us through the medium of people: what they think, what they say, and what they do. So, the best way to mount a response to system forces is through relationships: the right relationships with the right people. *(page 207)*

Tool • Use the map you drew of your systems (Chapter 18) to identify the strategic relationships most in need of cultivation and development. *(pages 208-210)*

Chapter 20. Big relationships, big results (page 213)

Idea • **Big results require big relationships** between you and the delegatee and among others the outcome relies upon. Big relationships are characterised by 1) mutual trust, 2) commitment, 3) honesty, and 4) communication. *(page 214)*

Reflection • What situations that your team encounters call for big relationships? If you can't think of any you may be coasting, stuck in routine, governed by the status quo.

Idea • Ineffective **co-created patterns** are cycles of